DISASTER
AT
39,000 FEET

Chicago

CENTERVILLE

IOWA

MISSOURI

ILLINOIS

UNIONVILLE

Kansas City

DISASTER AT 39,000 FEET

HOW SMALL-TOWN AMERICA CAME TOGETHER AT A TIME OF CRISIS

ENFYS MCMURRY

Enfys McMurry

Feb 24 2024

MEADOWLARK PRESS

Celebrating 10 Years
established 2014

EMPORIA, KANSAS

Meadowlark Press, LLC
meadowlarkbookstore.com
PO Box 333, Emporia, KS 66801

Disaster at 39,000 Feet:
How Small-Town America Came Together at a Time of Crisis
Copyright © 2024 Enfys McMurry

Cover & Interior: TMS, Meadowlark Press
Cover Design: Roger Griffing, Bill Buss, Jacquie Daly

This work is entirely factual. Information was pulled from CAB and FBI official reports, police log sheets, newspaper accounts, biographies, emails, and interviews by the author.

Ordering Information: Special discounts are available on quantity purchases by corporations, associations, and others. For details, contact the publisher at info@meadowlark-books.com.

TRANSPORTATION / Aviation / History
TRUE CRIME / Murder / Mass Murder
HISTORY / United States / State & Local / Midwest
HISTORY / United States / 20th Century

ISBN: 978-1-956578-53-9

Library of Congress Control Number: 2024931155

For the Families of the Victims
denotes flight crew member

Jack David Alexander
Dallas, Texas (POB: Enid, Oklahoma)

*Roger Dean Allen
Palos Verdes, California (POB: Genoa, Colorado)

Kenneth Howell Berger
Rochester, New York (POB: Buffalo, New York)

*Stella Ann Berry,
Los Angeles, California. (POB: Richland County, Wisconsin)

*Marilyn Irene Bloomquist
El Segundo, California

Donald Dalton Bowman
Merriam, Kansas (POB: Tiffin, Missouri)

Marcus Coleman Brand
Overland Park, Kansas (POB: Kansas City, Missouri)

Beuford Mack Carter
Alden, Kansas (POB: Bosworth, Missouri)

William Crouch Chapin
Rochester, New York (POB: Rochester, New York)

James Archibald Clarity Jr.
Des Plaines, Illinois (POB: Minneapolis, Minnesota)

Tommie Jefferson Cox
Meade, Kansas (POB: Des Moines, New Mexico)

Thomas Gene Doty
Merriam, Kansas (POB: San Antonio, Texas)

Geneva Opal Fraley
Independence, Missouri (POB: Camdenton, Missouri)

Clyde Darrel Fritz
Kansas City, Kansas (POB: Hartville, Missouri)

Robert Calvin Gach
Chicago, Illinois

Philip Eugene Giberson Sr.
Jackson, Michigan (POB: Muncie, Indiana)

Sidney Herbert Goldberg
Howlett Harbor, New York (POB: Belarus)

★Fred Rudolph Gray
Pacific Palisades. California (POB: Denver, Colorado)

Frank Joseph Grene Jr.
Minneapolis, Minnesota (POB: Chicago, Illinois)

Maurice Edward Hamilton
Cleveland, Ohio (POB: Youngstown, Ohio)

John Earl Hamm
Kansas City, Missouri (POB: Sedalia, Missouri)

Henry Evans Hanna
Lyons, Kansas (POB: Little River, Kansas)

Fred Paul Herman
Dearborn, Michigan (POB: Rokycanova, Czechoslovakia)

Philip Ireland Hoare
Surrey, England (POB: Cardiff, Wales)

Marvin Dale Horn
Independence, Missouri (POB: St. Edward, Nebraska)

Edward Arthur Kuhn
Aurora, Illinois. (POB: Walker, Iowa)

*Mary Rosalie McGrath
El Segundo, California (POB: Chicago, Illinois)

Robert Lee Miller
Fort Riley, Kansas (POB: Maywood, Illinois)

Virgil Wesley Mourning
Franklin, Michigan (POB Jerseyville, Illinois)

Takehiko Nakano
Evanston, Illinois (POB: Tokyo, Japan)

*David Eric Max Olssen
El Segundo, California (POB: Las Animas, Colorado)

Ross Addison Reid
US Navy, Detroit, Michigan (POB: Bay City, Michigan)

Andrew Peter Roucka
Chicago, Illinois (POB: Skokie, Illinois)

*Martha Joyce Rush
Manhattan Beach, California. (POB: Stamford, Texas)

Bruce Stewart
Des Plaines, Illinois (POB: Evanston, Illinois)

*Edward Joseph Sullivan
Inglewood, California (POB: Youngstown, Ohio)

Robert Gustav Tabors
Providence, Rhode Island (POB: Chicago, Illinois)

Rex Ora Thomas
Mount Prospect, Illinois (POB: Brazil, Indiana)

Benjamin Franklin Tuttle
Mount Prospect, Illinois. (POB: Neodesha, Kansas)

Edward Christian Waffle Jr.
North Kansas City, Missouri (Chicago, Illinois)

Clifford Lewis Walton
Laverne, Oklahoma. (POB: Coxs Mills, West Virginia)

James Raymond Webb
Anaheim, California (POB: Los Angeles, California)

Roger Welch
Grosse Pointe, Michigan (POB: Marshall, Michigan)

Bobby Jack Wilks
Durham, North Carolina (POB: Taylor, Texas)

Russell Warden Wolfe
Guymon, Oklahoma (POB: Robinson, Illinois)

For the people of Appanoose County, Iowa
For the people of Putnam County, Missouri

For those who told their stories:
Retired US Major Duane Crawford of Unionville, Missouri
Charles DePuy of the Centerville Daily Iowegian
Andrew Russell, aviation writer, author of The Missouri Crash

"This Will Go Down in Aviation History"
Civil Aeronautics Board Chief Investigator:
George Van Epps. May 30, 1962

Table of Contents

.

Captain Fred R. Gray

Tuesday, May 22, 1962

Chicago: O'Hare Airport
7:00 PM CT Tuesday

Continental Airlines Flight 10, one of Continental's Golden Jet luxury passenger aircraft, arrives from Los Angeles, California. Routine servicing and inspections prepare the aircraft for its turnaround flight back to Los Angeles with an intermediate stop in Kansas City. It is now Continental Aircraft N70775, Boeing 707-124, "The Champagne Flight": Continental Airlines Flight 11. [1]

7:13 PM CT Tuesday

Thirteen minutes later Continental Airlines Flight 4, a Boeing 720, also from Los Angeles, lands at Chicago O'Hare Airport. The crew of Flight 4 transfers to Continental Flight 11. Taking the left seat in Flight 11's cockpit is fifty-one-year-old Captain Fred Gray, a twenty-three-year veteran pilot for Continental with 23,000 hours of flying time—2,600 of those in a Boeing 707. Alongside are his co-pilot and First Officer, forty-one-year-old Edward Sullivan with a flying time of 14,500 hours—six-hundred in a Boeing 707, and Second Officer, thirty-two-year-old Roger Allen, the flight engineer and a pilot licensed to fly a 707. [1]

In the cabin, getting ready to greet passengers is the Director of Passenger Services, thirty-nine-year-old Dave Olssen. With him are four stewardesses: Marilyn Bloomquist, Mary McGrath, Martha Joyce Rush, and Stella Ann Berry. All four are immaculate in Continental's signature gold-colored uniforms and red berets. All four are under twenty-five years of age with the youngest, Stella Ann Berry, two weeks short of her twenty-first birthday. All are based in California. They are heading home. This is a happy crew. It always is when Captain Freddie Gray is in charge.[1, 2]

7:30 PM CT Tuesday

In the cockpit, Captain Gray is handed the proposed flight plan for Flight 11 by Continental's customer agent. The plan, dispatched at Continental's headquarters at Stapleton Field, Denver, Colorado, is for a one-hour, one-minute flying time to Kansas City at an altitude of 29,000 feet. With a clear sky in Chicago and an immediate visibility unlimited, the outlook is for a routine flight. But Captain Gray, aware of thunderstorm activity west of Chicago, scans a new report issued by the US Weather Bureau. It is a warning of a storm associated with an active cold front, pre-frontal squall lines, maximum tops of 50,000 feet with severe to extreme turbulence and the possibility of tornadoes. It lies across part of Continental Flight 11's flight plan. Captain Gray, experienced with such storms, changes Flight 11's proposed altitude to 39,000 feet. At the same time, he warns the cabin crew of possible turbulence ahead. The storm, says the report, is currently in the vicinity of Centerville, Iowa.[1]

Three-hundred fifty miles west: Centerville, Iowa
7:30 PM CT Tuesday

In Centerville, warnings of severe storms have been out over radio stations since noon. Charlie DePuy the Managing Editor of *The Centerville Daily Iowegian* is driving the fifty-four miles from Kirksville, Missouri, back home to Centerville. He is tired. Robert Beck, the newspaper's Editor and Publisher is on a well-earned vacation in Hot Springs, Arkansas. Charlie is working double time. Since mid-afternoon he and his wife Gladys have delivered newspapers seven miles from Centerville to Exline, five miles to Cincinnati (Iowa), thirteen more across the Missouri State line to Unionville in Putnam County and another thirty-nine miles to Kirksville. And all the way, Charlie and Gladys have fought the storms: first clear skies and sunshine, then dark clouds, downbursts of rain and hail, the two of them watching for the rotating clouds of a tornado. Writing about the weather this day, Charlie uses the word "sinister." Perhaps prophetically. At 7:30 PM Charlie has reached Unionville, Missouri. Another storm breaks. He drives north onto Highway 5 (Iowa Highway 60). Ahead in Iowa the clouds are clearing. He'll be home in twenty minutes. He anticipates a good night's rest.[3]

Chicago: O'Hare Airport
8:00 PM CT Tuesday

Now boarding Flight 11 are thirty-five passengers. Continental Airlines Departure Agent, twenty-one-year-old Ralph Boester relays their information, their seat assignments, meal requirements and their baggage to the operations side of the aircraft. The passengers come from twenty states and three foreign countries. Most are businessmen: entrepreneurs, executives, accountants, members of a team ready to install natural gas transmission lines, and officials of the Chrysler/Dodge Corporation. Twenty-nine of the thirty-five have served their nation at a time of war: sixteen in World War II and another three in Korea. Five are members of the National Defense Program and one, a twenty-one-year-old ascending the stairs in his military uniform, is returning to service at Ft. Riley, Kansas, after a furlough with his family in Chicago. All are welcomed aboard, guided to their assigned seats and made comfortable. The doors are closed. The stairs removed. Two late passengers are seen running for the flight. One, a woman, the other, her male companion. They hold tickets for Kansas City. The man is carrying a brown leather briefcase. Continental Gatekeeper Tom Duley orders the stairs replaced. The door reopens and the two board. Flight 11's forward flight attendant hands Tom Duley a cup of fresh coffee, smiles and wishes him a good night. The door recloses. The stairs are removed. Flight 11 taxies. It is airborne at 8:35 PM. In the Continental Airlines office on the eighteenth floor of the Precious Gems Building in downtown Chicago, Ralph Boester forwards his information and records of Flight 11 to Kansas City Municipal Airport via teletype. [4, 5, 6, 7]

Unionville, Missouri
8:30 PM CT Tuesday

Enjoying an evening drive around Unionville are Leo and Barbara Craver with their good friends Jack and Judy Morris. Between storms the four have driven down from Centerville, looking at new homes in Exline and Cincinnati, many built with materials bought at Leo's successful Craver Lumber Company on Centerville's Highway 2. They have driven south across the Missouri State line to Unionville. On Main Street across from the Unionville Power Plant they are enjoying an evening meal and sheltering from another storm in Beulah's Place a popular Unionville restaurant. [9]

Two doors east of Beulah's Place, David Fowler, the Sheriff of Putnam County, and his wife Hazelee are playing cards in the home of their friends Don and Frances Shuey. The evening storm is beginning to abate, but there's still thunder and it's a hot and humid evening. The windows and doors of the Shuey home are open wide. [10, 11]

Don and Frances Shuey own a farm six miles north and west of Unionville. They are renting it to Terry and Edna Bunnell. It's good land with an oat field, an eight-acre cornfield where a new crop is starting to emerge. And there's a gently sloping hay field, a line of trees fringing its edge where Terry's thirty dairy cows graze on grass rich with alfalfa. On this evening Terry and Edna are celebrating their wedding anniversary with their one-year-old daughter Rhonda and with Terry's sister Shirley and her husband, Gene Crawford.

Their nearest neighbors lie one mile in each direction: to the east Cleo and Ila Jean Webber; to the west Lester and Atholene Cook and their three children: Ronnie (seventeen) Marla (fifteen) and Marilyn (eleven).[12, 13]

Aurora, Illinois
8:52 PM CT Tuesday

From the moment of take-off, Continental Flight 11 is being monitored at the Chicago Air Traffic Control Center in Aurora. Seventeen minutes into the flight, the craft is reported flying west at 39,000 feet on Jet Route 26 Victor over Bradford, Illinois.[1]

Just east of the Mississippi River
9:01 PM CT Tuesday

Captain Gray requests the Chicago Center for a radar picture of the squall line he'll encounter in Iowa. Chicago hands the request over to the Federal Aviation Administration's Controller at the 788 Radar Squadron Station in Waverly, north of Waterloo, Iowa.[1]

Waverly, Iowa
9:02 PM CT Tuesday

The FAA Controller in Waverly is closely reading his circular radar screen. He's currently tracking the flight path of an Air France aircraft. With the transfer of Continental Flight 11 from Chicago, he begins following Flight 11's path and writing its movements onto "progress strips" he slips alongside into a rack. On duty near the Controller, nineteen-year-old Airman First Class Carl McCarthy is checking transmitter accuracy. The Controller tells Captain Gray he can anticipate not one squall line but three. "It's about a toss-up between north and south," Waverly continues. "About your present position or maybe a 260 or 270 compass heading, possibly a 260 would be a little bit better and would go through the hole to the north." "Let's try that one," Flight 11 responds, "We're heading 260."[1, 14, 15]

9:10 PM CT Tuesday

Eight minutes later, Captain Gray reports that Flight 11 has successfully passed around the storm cell. Waverly's Controller responds, "I show just about from your present position direct to Kirksville now should clear all weather." "Okay," says Flight 11, "Requesting our present position direct [to] Kansas City." He tells Waverly he's starting a turn from 270° to 247° and thirty seconds later to 230°. And Captain Gray begins a normal descent from 39,000 at 9:14 PM continuing at a normal rate of 1,000 feet per minute for two minutes and seven seconds.[1, 16]

The Iowa/Missouri border
9:15 PM CT Tuesday

One mile south of the border, across from the Haas Black Kettle Restaurant, Claude "Junior" Johnson is preparing to lock the Shields gas station for the night. Accompanying him is his friend Tom McKay. North of the border at Cincinnati's telephone exchange, Marjorie Jones has taken her place for night duty. She is raising the blind to watch her husband Carl drive away. Six miles to the west on a farm south of Livingston, fourteen-year-old Sharon Smith is watching television with her family and celebrating her eighth-grade graduation from Seymour School. Seven miles to the northeast, John Koestner is leaving the Bluebird Café he runs on the south side of Centerville Square and begins his walk to his home on Maple Street. Just off the east side of Centerville Square at the Elks Club, Putnam County's popular doctor, Charles Judd, is finishing his weekly meal of fried oysters. He is preparing to drive back south along Highway 5 to his home in Unionville. At the same time leaving Beulah's Place in Unionville and beginning their drive north along Highway 5 (IA 60) back home to Centerville are Leo and Barbara Craver and Jack and Judy Morris. They are admiring the beautiful evening—so clear, so starlit, so calm, so serene after the storms of the day.[17, 18, 19]

Waverly, Iowa
9:15 PM CT Tuesday

The Waverly Controller reports to Captain Gray that the Kansas City Center is slow responding to the captain's request for descent. "Okay" responds Flight 11—"We can probably reach them on your radio. Do you want to send us over?"[1]

9:16 PM CT Tuesday

Waverly gives radio communication for Flight 11 to Kansas City Center on 133.95 mcs. At this moment Kansas City responds and Waverly gives a radar handoff for Flight 11: The aircraft is flying ten miles south of the Intersections of Airways J45V and J64V and moving in a southerly direction.[1]

9:17 PM CT Tuesday

The Kansas City Controller observes an indistinct target at this position. Then the target fades. After two or three sweeps of the antenna, there is nothing. At the same time Waverly watches the aircraft's transponder return . . . and that too fades. The Waverly Controller shouts: "Flight 11! Flight 11!" There is no response. To Airman First Class Carl McCarthy he says, "He's gone! He's gone!"[1, 15]

Flight 11 has disappeared.

The time is 9:17 and 7 seconds Central Standard Time.

The Iowa/Missouri Border
9:17.7 PM CT Tuesday

One mile south of the border, Junior Johnson has just locked the Shields gas station for the night. He is walking to the adjoining restaurant to meet his wife Joethea and walk home to join their three children. He stops . . . "Look at that!" he says to Tom McKay . . . "Not a cloud in the sky—but lightning."[17]

North of the border at Cincinnati's telephone exchange, Marjorie Jones is sitting at the switchboard looking out of the window to the west side of the square. She sees a flash of blue light so bright an instant second of brilliant daylight outlines the roof lines and the branches of the trees without shadow. "That's not lightning," she thinks—"it's more like fireworks." And it is silent. No sound. No thunder. Her phone rings, it's Vivian Stickler: "I was outside," she tells Marjorie, ". . . and I saw a flash in the sky as big as a house and to the south."

Six miles west, Sharon Smith with her parents is watching television. The set stands to the left of the south-facing large picture window. There's a bright, brilliant flash of light. Sharon looks at her parents. They thought the storm was over. Together they look outside. The sky is clear.

In Centerville, John Koestner has reached his home on Maple Street. His family is watching the Emmy Awards on television. So is Gary Craver, a student at Centerville Community College, at home on North Haynes Avenue where his mother Marguerite is wall papering a bedroom. John Koestner calls his family out onto the porch to view the stars and the clear evening. Then his son Kris sees "a brilliant light, just for a second. It is all around and everywhere."[3, 19, 20]

A B-47 Stratojet bomber flying from Forbes Air Base in Topeka, Kansas, is currently flying north of Kirksville, Missouri, at 26,500 feet. The commander sees a bright flash in the sky forward of and above his position. He checks his navigation logs. He records the time, the weather in the area: "clear with little or no turbulence." He notes the place. He's approaching Lake Wapello in Iowa's Davis County. The lake is thirty-five miles northeast of Centerville. It is forty miles northeast of a gently sloping hay field in northern Putnam County, Missouri.[1]

In the same eastern part of Appanoose County some eight miles west of Lake Wapello on rural road J3T, Jeanne Harrington is preparing for bed. The sound she hears is so sudden, so loud, so deafening, she falls to the floor.[21]

The Appanoose/Putnam Counties Border
9:21.15 PM CT Tuesday

There are more reports of sounds. These occur four minutes later and forty miles southwest of Lake Wapello. Ted Corder calls Marjorie Jones at Cincinnati's telephone exchange: "Where was that car crash?" Girls at the Loyal Workers Sunday school party at Virge Allison's house hear the noise and think they'll be walking home in another storm, but they find a night that is clear and still. So does Cincinnati's Town Marshall, Lloyd Richmond, who goes outside after his daughter screams on hearing two loud sounds. Thirteen miles across the state border to the south, sounds are heard in Unionville, Missouri. Mrs. Junior Rollins describes them as large claps "like thunder." Sheriff David Fowler playing cards at the Shuey home describes hearing "a boom." Others say a "popping" sound. Mr. & Mrs. Emerson Tysor say it is a "swish and then a boom boom."[22]

But it's six miles to the northwest of Unionville, three miles south of the Iowa border where, for three neighboring families—the Bunnells, the Cooks, and the Webbers—the sounds are the loudest, the longest, the most powerful. There, surrounding the Shuey land, the sloping land, the one with a tree line fringe at its edge, the hay field where the grass grows rich with alfalfa. On the north side of the alfalfa-rich hay field, the Bunnells are entertaining their friends, the Crawfords. They are eating supper. There is a rumbling sound. It comes from the south. It lasts ten seconds. The ground trembles. The windows rattle. The house shakes as if dynamite has exploded.[13, 31]

A mile west of the field, seventeen-year-old Ronnie Cook is drifting to sleep. He hears a sound, "a loud dreadful sound." Fifteen-year-old Marla working on her homework in the living room hears it too: an "eerie sound . . . UFO eerie." Eleven-year-old Marilyn on her top bunk bed is reading. Ronnie and Marla go outside. They see nothing but a clear still starlit night. Marilyn holds close her little dog, Mitzi.[22, 23]

At the top of the alfalfa hay field Terry Bunnell and Gene Crawford are outside looking for the source of the noise. Gene thinks the sound is like he imagines an air crash would be, but everywhere is quiet. Everything is still. The two men reason together: so many jets fly over this part of rural Missouri, sonic booms are frequent. Terry recalls the window-shattering sonic booms that shake him when he's driving his tractor. The Cooks, too, consider the sound to be a sonic boom. Marilyn, the youngest of the Cook family, remembers sonic booms that hurt the ears and one in particular that shattered the screen of their television set. The Webbers living one mile to the east hear the thunderous booms but consider them the approach of another storm. Everything is quiet and still and peaceful. All three families retire for the night.[13, 32, 33]

Washington DC
10:30 PM Eastern Time Tuesday

Two Washington DC offices—the Civil Aeronautics Board (CAB) on Dupont Circle and the Federal Aviation Agency★ (FAA) on Independence Avenue are immediately informed of the disappearance from radar of Flight 11. So is the Headquarters of Continental Airlines on Stapleton Field in Denver, Colorado. The aircraft's last transmission is of vital importance: "Ten miles south of the intersection of Airways J45 and J64V and moving in a southerly direction." This places Captain Gray in the seventy-mile segment between Fort Madison, Iowa, and Kirksville, Missouri. At two radar stations, Waverly and Kansas City operators are triangulating their information with Jeppesen Aeronautical Navigation Charts and land maps. They determine Flight 11 is well to the west of Fort Madison. It is on the ground somewhere in the vicinity of Centerville, Iowa. There is no contact with the aircraft. Its exact location is unknown.[1]

*The Federal Aviation Agency was changed to Federal Aviation Administration in 1967.

Five miles south of Centerville, Iowa
9:20 PM CT Tuesday

After their dinner in Unionville, Missouri, Leo and Barbara Craver, Jack and Judy Morris are driving home north along Highway 5 (IA 60). At the Exline turnoff, five miles south of Centerville, they see a scattering of debris, and on the roadway a large piece of bent metal. Two cars ahead of them drive wide around it. So does Dr. Judd, driving home south to Unionville after his oyster dinner at Centerville's Elks Club. Leo and Jack stop. They go back and examine the metal in the headlights of their car. It is aluminum, three feet long, six inches wide, green on one side, gray on the other, and there are rivets—smooth round rivets—distinctive rivets—aircraft rivets. Leo is a World War II veteran. For three years he served in the US Army/Air Force Medical Rescue Corps conducting aerial vigilance over the vitally strategic Panama Canal. He has taken part in thirty to forty aircraft accident investigations—both American and Japanese, and Leo knows a piece of an aircraft when he sees it. "We'd better take this to the police station," he tells Jack. Deputy Police Chief Curtis Green, on dispatcher duty, contacts Centerville Airport. "Nothing unusual here and no news of any aircraft incident anywhere," is the report. Appanoose County Sheriff Paul Thomas arrives. Leo is a member of his posse. He knows Leo's background, and he knows Leo's judgment. "Let's go back and you show me where you found this." They head back south to the Exline turnoff. The sheriff, the Cravers, and the Morrises are joined by two Iowa highway patrol officers, James Douglas and Bill Pickard.[34, 35]

Mountain View, California
7:30 PM Pacific Time Tuesday

Najeeb Halaby, the Head of the FAA appointed by President John F. Kennedy a year earlier, is studying new aircraft wing designs at the Ames Laboratory, Moffett Air Force Base, Mountain View, California. The FAA office in Washington DC contacts him with the news. Halaby boards an FAA Gulfstream N1 and begins the flight through the night to Centerville.[36]

Denver, Colorado
8:30 PM Mountain Time Tuesday

At the headquarters of Continental Airlines at Stapleton Airfield, Denver, Colorado, Harding Lawrence, the Executive Vice-President of Continental, is making a trans-Atlantic telephone call to Robert "Bob" Six, Continental's Chief Executive Officer.[2]

A hotel in Paris, France
4:30 AM Central European Time

Bob Six is asleep. He responds to the continual ringing of the telephone and goes to an adjoining room. His wife, the actress Audrey Meadows (star of *the Honeymooners* television series), sensing bad news, orders coffee. Harding Lawrence tells Six one of Continental's 707s is missing and could have fallen apart in a storm. "Who was the

Captain?" "Fred Gray." "Don't give me that!" says Six, "Freddie Gray would never let himself get caught in a killer storm." The Sixes pack and leave for New York on the first available flight at noon Paris time. From New York, Six will fly on alone to Kansas City and from there to Centerville.[2]

Five miles south of Centerville
9:30 PM CT Tuesday

Sheriff Paul Thomas, two highway patrol officers, Leo and Barbara Craver, and Jack and Judy Morris arrive back at the Exline turnoff. Dozens of people are out. They are on both sides of the road. They are in the fields. They are carrying flashlights, moving like fireflies through the dark. They are picking up paper napkins, paper cups, a spoon, a knife, pieces of metal. In a shale driveway Leo is handed a three-by-four foot section of plywood. On the reverse, rammed into a crack, Leo extracts a paper. He reads, "Continental Airlines Flight 11. Chicago to Kansas City." There's a seat number and there's a name. At this news a highway patrol officer immediately contacts his division headquarters in Des Moines. A new report has just been received. "A passenger airliner with thirty-seven passengers and eight crew is overdue at Kansas City and is missing from radar. Its last known location is somewhere in the vicinity of Centerville, Iowa." Centerville Police Assistant Chief Curtis Green is announcing on police radio, "We think we have a plane down south of town."[9]

Then, in the words of Al Clark reading a newspaper four hours into his 24-hour night shift at the Centerville Fire Rescue Station—"All Hell breaks loose."[37, 38]

Washington DC
11:00 PM Eastern Time Tuesday

A CAB team of six experts prepares to leave for Centerville. In charge of the team, CAB's Head of Safety Investigation and the nation's chief expert on Boeing 707 jet aircraft, George A. Van Epps. With Van Epps is CAB's Public Relations Information Officer: Edward E. Slattery, Jr.[38]

Prairie Village, Kansas
10:02 PM CT Tuesday

Dewey Ballard is on accident duty for the FAA in Kansas City. He gets a call from the Kansas City Airport. Flight 11 is twenty-four minutes overdue and is missing from radar. Ballard, himself an aviator and a World War II veteran, needs no more. A 707 doesn't just disappear. He collects a team and heads out to Centerville.

The Arrivals Gate at Kansas City Airport
10:12 PM CT Tuesday

Flight 11 is late. Over half an hour late. Thirty-three of Continental Flight 11's thirty-seven passengers are due to disembark in Kansas City before the jet continues on to Los Angeles. Waiting to greet them are family members, friends, and business associates. One or two approach the ticket counter. Others draw together in taut groups. A few minutes before 10:15 PM, a voice on a public-address system requests those waiting for Flight 11 to go to the President's Club Lounge. Henry Hague, Continental's ticket counter supervisor addresses them: "There is difficulty in contacting the plane." In the silence that follows, a woman speaks, "If you hear something, I won't worry . . . It's the not hearing makes me worry."[40]

Chicago, O'Hare Airport
10:15 PM CT Tuesday

Twenty-one-year-old Ralph Boester, Continental's Chicago Forwarding Agent, is preparing to go home. As a matter of routine, he checks the status of his shift's last take-off, which was Flight 11. "When was the last time you heard anything from Flight 11?" Flight Control replies, "Fifteen or twenty minutes." Soon it was thirty minutes. Boester wakes his manager.[41]

Waverly, Iowa
10:17 PM CT Tuesday

Two Federal Bureau of Investigation agents from Waterloo are arriving at the 788 Radar Squadron Station. They are cross-examining the FAA Controller, challenging his tracking record of Flight 11. They remove the black box from the equipment and the FAA Controller leaves with them. [15]

Centerville, Iowa
10:15 PM CT Tuesday

Across Centerville telephones are ringing. Persistently. Voices are raised, the message urgent: Get south of town as fast as you can to search for a missing airliner and many passengers. The calls go to the fire department, to Curtis Green at the adjacent police station, to the civil defense members. There are calls for the posse truck and for emergency lighting. Off-duty fireman Gene Horn, at his home in Moulton, hears the messages on the citizens band radio he keeps on all night. The two funeral homes: the Miller-Wehrle on West State Street and the Johnson Funeral Home on Maple Street are told to stand by, to coordinate with St. Joseph Mercy Hospital, local physicians, and with Bob Buss, the head of Hall Engineering for three vehicles to extend the limited capacity of single station-wagon ambulances. Al Clark at the fire department has already prepared the department's panel rescue truck with its three-bed capacity.

By this time neighbors are calling neighbors. Volunteers are leaving their beds. And on his strip farm east of Centerville, a phone call eliminates all hope of good early night's sleep for Charlie DePuy, the *Daily Iowegian's* Managing Editor. "Say—there's something about a plane being wrecked or something," says a voice. "You'd better investigate. I think it might be something big." Charlie and Gladys grab a camera and head south out of town.[36, 42, 43, 44, 45, 46]

Across town to the west at his home on North First Street, Dr. Eugene Ritter answers his phone. It's his partner, Dr. Elmer Larsen: "There's some sort of air crash south of town." For Dr. Ritter, it's difficult to think of a more suitable individual for this moment, this place, this event. Now close to retirement, he's known as a brilliant doctor, a local boy, one whose skills and personality have been honed in war. In World War II he spent four years on New Guinea. There he ran a field hospital performing emergency surgeries under palm trees with his assistant, Hollywood star and conscientious objector, Lew Ayres, and was battalion surgeon at the 54th US Army Hospital, the largest outside the continental US. Ritter is direct, forceful, suffers no fools and takes command without effort. He is also the FAA's Regional Aviation Medical Examiner. He collects his medical equipment and drives to Cincinnati.[47, 48, 49, 50]

Highway 5 South of Centerville
10:30 PM CT Tuesday

The whole area south of Centerville is aroused. Police cars and highway patrol cars are operating up and down the highway. From the Exline turnoff to Cincinnati there are search parties with walkie-talkies and flashlights, individuals with torches, vehicles shining spotlights. People are in ditches and in isolated tracks and on every side road, wet and muddy from the day's storms. They are following a trail of debris that tags Highway 5 in a steady southwest direction. Their discoveries are ominous. Two blood-stained pillows. Sandwiches with blood on them. Cups. Bits of metal. An escape hatch door. A spoon and a knife found on Cincinnati's Main Street. And no sign of an aircraft.[3]

Cincinnati, Iowa
10:45 PM CT Tuesday

Charlie DePuy, the inexhaustible newspaper man, arrives in Cincinnati. From Marjorie Jones's telephone office, he phones national news agencies to let them know what is happening. They already know. The story is across the country. Marjorie Jones is already overwhelmed. The first incoming call is from a Centerville operator to Charlie: "Get back here and answer the myriad of calls we have coming in." Gladys, Charlie's wife, stays with Marjorie. Charlie returns to the trail. He promises to come back at intervals to take press and radio calls and keep them up to date.[51, 52]

Cincinnati, Iowa
11:00 PM CT Tuesday

Across Cincinnati Square, Dr. Ritter is viewing a piece of discovered metal. It lies blocking the highway. He identifies the type of aircraft and its size. They are consistent with the object of the search. He contacts the FAA and CAB offices in Kansas City. He gives the precise ground geographic location of the search and its southwest projection. Hot coffee arrives from Bert and Bill's Café and Lyle Wells's Dairy Sweet. Anticipating the need for more coffee and possibly for food, Barbara Craver and Judy Morris drive north to Centerville's Green Circle Restaurant. "This is going to be a long night," they tell owner, Louie Sacco. "Start the coffee."[3, 53, 54]

On Highway 60 (#5) South of Cincinnati, Iowa
11:30 PM CT Tuesday

A phalanx of some two-hundred people is moving south. At the lead is Appanoose Sheriff Paul Thomas. Following are eighteen members of his posse, among them Leo Craver who found the first piece of metal from Flight 11, Gary Barrickman from the Craver Lumber Company, and Wilbur Rush from Centerville National Bank. Following too are the police, civil defense members, ambulances, firemen, and highway patrol officers—one of them Sgt. James Douglas, walking next to Dr. Ritter. New volunteers arrive. Ritter tells the sheriff to instruct every searcher to leave any discovered item unmolested and to remember its location to assist later investigators. He orders the Centerville National Guard to be on standby and prepare a morgue at the National Guard Armory on Centerville's West Franklin Street.[33, 42, 56]

Further south on Highway 60(#5)
11:50 PM CT Tuesday

The progress south of Cincinnati is slow. The searchers explore the sides of the road. They cross into adjacent fields. They follow every cart track. More and more pieces of the aircraft are being found. To Charlie DePuy moving alongside in his car recording each discovery, it is some gargantuan and macabre hare and hounds chase. To Curtis Green, Centerville's Deputy Police Chief, "It's frustrating. We keep finding parts of it, parts of wings, parts of fuselage, pieces of the inside. Just like you'd blown it to bits." One of the volunteers, Dr. Pat Gleason—for twenty-four years a Centerville optometrist—agrees: "We keep finding plane parts. I picked up one with fresh blood. I told the others, this is a major tragedy. We just keep working to the southwest . . . but no wreckage . . . It seems everyone is searching."[42, 55]

The discoveries are becoming larger and ever more ominous: an inner door labeled "To Be Opened on Take-off and Landing." A pulley. Part of an aircraft galley. A piece of metal painted white with red and blue stripes. A lavatory with blood. An eight-foot section of fuselage. A cupboard still containing cups and dishes. An outer door bearing Continental's insignia of an eagle. But still no aircraft. No passengers. No crew. No victims.[42]

Charlie keeps his word. From time to time through this long night he returns to the Cincinnati telephone office. Each time there are calls waiting: CBS, the *Chicago American*, the *Chicago News*, Detroit, New York, Associated Press, United Press. Multiple radio stations call: "Will you give us a first-hand statement, count to ten (or five) and start talking." One call comes from the radio station in Mojave, California. Another from Oelwein, Iowa. Charlie always gives the same response: ". . . the hills and darkness of the Iowa-Missouri border still hold their tragic secret."[3, 51, 57]

Wednesday, May 23, 1962

Unionville, Missouri
12:01 AM CT Wednesday

For some time the police dispatcher on night-duty at the Unionville Power Plant has been receiving telephone calls: "What's happening up in Iowa?" Local radio stations are carrying the national news reports, including interviews with Charlie DePuy. The calls get increasingly specific: "Something is going on south of Centerville" . . . "They're out in force south of Cincinnati" . . . and . . . "hundreds of people are approaching the Missouri border." The dispatcher contacts the sheriff of Putnam County.[29]

Directly across Main Street from the Unionville Power Plant, Sheriff David Fowler and his wife Hazelee are finishing their card game with their friends Don and Frances Shuey. At the dispatcher's news, all four immediately drive north to the border. The car radio is covering the story . . . an airliner is missing . . . it has disappeared from radar . . . it's a Boeing 707 . . . there are many passengers . . . it is believed to be somewhere near Centerville, Iowa. At the border they are joined by Unionville's Mayor and co-editor of the *Unionville Republican* newspaper, Aaron Stuckey. Through the trees to the north, they see flashes of lights, searchers moving through the darkness. The odor of airplane fuel is strong. It is stronger here, three miles south of the border. For Sheriff Fowler, action is needed. It is needed urgently.[59]

Kansas City Municipal Airport
12:27 AM CT Wednesday

It has been two hours since Continental's last announcement about Flight 11 to those waiting for its arrival. Most have stayed in the President's Club Lounge. A few have left. At 12:27 AM Henry Hague, Continental's ticket supervisor, gathers them together. "Folks," he says, "we still have only sketchy information. We do know that the aircraft is down, just north of Cincinnati, Iowa, but we don't know the disposition of the plane or the passengers. We will call you immediately if you want to go home . . . it might be two or three hours before they know anything. Any questions?" A woman in a bright yellow dress asks the only question: "Why would it take so long?" Another woman leaves the lounge quietly. She goes to a telephone and gives an account of the situation. She asks: "Do you want me to stay here or come home? I guess there's not much I can do anywhere."[40]

Highway 60 (#5) Approaching the Missouri Border
1:00 AM CT Wednesday

Three miles south of Cincinnati, Little Shoal Creek accepts four tributaries from the northwest. Tonight, after the storms of the day, these tributaries are full, overflowing through a rough terrain of hills, forests where tree branches hang low, and bushes are thick with thorns. It is here the path of debris from Flight 11 leaves the highway and crosses southwest over open countryside. It is here Gene Horn and the Centerville Fire Department team follow the trail. Their path is impeded, slowed by the undergrowth, hampered as they wade through waist-high mud. Through the dark they see scattered bright clothing spilling from broken luggage. Then suddenly, in an unexpected glade between trees, Gene finds an aircraft wing. A wing: twenty-nine feet in length, its ailerons flipped up, lying over its outboard edge. The odor of aircraft fuel is strong. The wreckage cannot be far.[60]

Unionville, Missouri
1:30 AM CT Wednesday

The Putnam County Dispatcher's message to Sheriff Fowler was at 12:01 AM. In response to his actions, the Unionville Power Plant is made the nerve center for all activity and information. In less than an hour, Missouri's highway patrol officers, Unionville Police and Fire Department, are reporting to Sheriff Fowler at the border. They are coordinating their search for Flight 11 with the Iowans searching north of the border. Some are working as far north as Cincinnati, guarding major pieces of the aircraft wreckage. But of the craft it-self—there is still no sign.[29]

Six miles northwest of Unionville, Missouri
2:20 AM CT Wednesday

Sheriff Fowler is shining his twin car floodlights and blowing his horn at the home of Lester and Atholene Cook. It wakes the house-hold. "There's an aircraft down somewhere near here," the sheriff tells Lester, "I need help to find it." "Go back to bed," Atholene tells Marla and Marilyn. Lester leaves with seventeen-year-old Ronnie. Mitzi, Marilyn's little dog panicking at the excitement runs away. Mrs. Cook telephones their neighbor Terry Bunnell. It isn't long after the Bunnells and the Crawfords have fallen asleep. "There could be an aircraft down on your land."[61, 62]

The Iowa/Missouri Borderland
2:30 AM CT Wednesday

There are seven hundred people searching for Continental Flight 11. These are on both sides of the border. Some in groups. Some search alone. Two hundred of them, one organized group, is the Center-ville phalanx: the ambulances, the rescue trucks, the police, fire department, highway patrol officers, Dr. Eugene Ritter, and Charlie DePuy noting events in preparation for that day's edition of the

Centerville Daily Iowegian newspaper. At their lead is Appanoose County Sheriff Paul Thomas and his posse. They are approaching the state borderline, Iowa #60 and Missouri #5.[51]

Some miles to the north Lester Ballard, the lead investigator for the FAA in Kansas City has arrived with his team. They find a trail of torn twisted metal that suggests a direction to follow. They pass metal shards and bloody airplane blankets. Ballard sees a body—it's hanging in a tree—a line of trees fringing an alfalfa hay field—a man's body, eyes open, intestines exposed, no clothes but socks, and an identity bracelet. Ballard reads the name: Doty. Ballard assigns one of his crew to stay with the body while the search continues.

Heading further southwest after his discovery of one of Flight 11's wings, Gene Horn finds an aircraft fuel tank. It is empty.[39, 43]

The Shuey land
2:45 AM CT Wednesday

As they leave their home, Lester and Ronnie remember the sound in the night. It came from the east. They head in that direction. They walk through weeds that are tall and wet. They climb fences. They cross a deep creek.

Terry Bunnell and Gene Crawford, awake since Atholene Cook's telephone call, have started hiking to the south. They, too, remember the direction of the sound in the night.

Lester and Ronnie are walking uphill . . . up the sloping hay field. The field where a line of trees fringes its edge. The one where the grass grows rich with alfalfa. That's where Ronnie first sees it . . . moonlight on metal and glass . . . the broken wreck of Continental Flight 11 . . . and there's nothing . . . nothing but silence . . . then moaning . . . a silence . . . moaning again. "We need help," says Lester.

A car is moving fast on the south dirt road. Ronnie rushes to stop it. Two newsmen are out searching. One is a reporter from KSO, a

CBS radio station in Des Moines. The other, a photographer. "Go with the driver," Lester tells Ronnie.

Terry Bunnell and Gene Crawford are walking for a mile across muddy fields. They cross down to what at first Terry thinks is a pile of logs. Then he sees the tangled mass of wreckage. It's resting on the slope of a shallow gully. And there isn't a sound . . . nothing but moonlight . . . and then moaning. Gene Crawford hurries back to the Bunnell farmhouse to call for help . . . to notify the world.[29, 63, 64, 65]

The Missouri State Line
3:00 AM CT Wednesday

The Centerville team of medics and rescuers have reached the border. They are waiting patiently for permission to enter Missouri. They are also waiting for one of their team, Byron Evans, Centerville's new postmaster who is also a pilot. Earlier, Byron has left to fly over the area, locate Flight 11, dip his wings to those at the border and fly indicating the direction of the crash site. Those waiting realize they have been up all night. At this moment Barbara Craver, Judy Morris, and Louie Sacco arrive from Centerville's Green Circle restaurant. They bring hot coffee and ham sandwiches. This is their third trip. Everything from Louie is donated.[30, 63]

The Missouri State Line
3:30 AM CT Wednesday

The KSO news reporter knows the Centerville rescue crew and medics are waiting at the border. He is driving Ronnie three miles on a dirt road and then north on Highway 5. Those waiting see a mud-covered car arriving, the driver emerging and shouting, pointing to Ronnie, "This kid has found the wreck with his dad." At this news, Ronnie sees the waiting crowd "go berserk." Charlie DePuy, his newsman acumen in full force, is up at the front. He hears talk of the Shuey land, the sound of a crash in the night. To Charlie "that almost clinches it. The wreck is probably on the Shuey farm rented by the Bunnells . . ." Camera in hand, Charlie takes off on his own. So too does Leo Craver. The crowd, the ambulances, and the rescue trucks follow Ronnie. They cross into Missouri, down Highway 5, a turn right—to the west—on a dirt road. Ronnie still leads. They walk and drive across fields, then Ronnie points north and says, "It's over the hill there." The crowd takes off, vehicles spinning their tires in the mud, fishtailing, creating ruts as they go fast for the miles of cross country.[42, 51, 64]

The Shuey Land
3:35 AM CT Wednesday

In response to Gene Crawford's telephone call the first help has arrived: a Missouri highway patrol officer with Bob Fowler, the sheriff's brother. With Bob is Robert, Bob's seven-year-old son. They see the wreck. Robert climbs onto the tip of the one existing wing. It is moist with rain. It shimmers silver in the moonlight. He walks its length. He sees hanging straps, thousands of wires, a scattering of pink. And he sees the pilot, his jacket immaculately folded over a chair back. And something from the pilot . . . something from his chest . . . something lying across the next seat.[66, 67]

Between Highway 5 and the Shuey Land
3:45 AM CT Wednesday

Charlie DePuy on his own in the dark is trudging through wet grass and brush finding his own way to the crash site. He climbs fences, falls over, tears his clothes, comes to a stream too wide to leap, aims for a rock in the middle, jumps, doesn't fall. He moves on through the dark through pastures, plowed ground, thick woods and more brush. One mile, two miles, maybe three. The first streaks of dawn begin to appear. If it isn't here . . . he thinks he's made a mistake . . . he'll have to reroute himself and go back. He reaches the brow of a hill and there ahead of him he sees the great hull, nose gone, tail gone, engines gone . . . but the long mid-section almost completely intact.[42]

Leo Craver, too, is making his own path from Highway 5. He reaches the wreckage. There . . the hull sitting in the middle of an alfalfa field . . . serene, still, silent, the missing tail an open wound. And all around it's "the prettiest spring morning imaginable . . . birds are singing, the countryside is fresh, calm, peaceful, beautiful." But Leo knows in that plane there is death. He knows what to expect.[9]

Airborne over the search area
4:15 AM CT Wednesday

It is Byron Evans's second flight. He's flying Brad Young's white high-wing Cessna aircraft. He was airborne first with Fred Clayton, Centerville airport's manager. That was at 1:30 AM. The moon is so bright this night, Byron thought he'd locate Flight 11 if the wreck was on a hillside. No luck. Now at 4:00 AM he's flying again. With him this time is Jack Morris who with Leo Craver had found the piece of metal on the highway, the first evidence of Continental Flight 11's fate. Byron is flying a zigzag course in a southwesterly direction from Centerville Airport. At 4:15 AM he sees the wreck. He sees a couple of people standing at the site. He radios the airport. He talks to local police. He tells them he'll circle the wreckage until the first car arrives. At the same time he's contacted by an FAA Gulfstream N1 aircraft arriving from California. Its passenger is Najeeb Halaby, the head of the FAA. Halaby requests Byron direct him to the scene.[68, 69]

The Crash Site
4:30 AM CT Wednesday

After directing Halaby's plane, Byron Evans is circling above the Shuey field. He sees the first rescue car arrive. It's the Centerville

Fire Department's high panel rescue truck. Behind it, the ambulances, the police, the highway patrol, the defense corps, the Appanoose Sheriff and his posse, and forty-four members of the Iowa National Guard, led by Sgt. Charles McCoy, all from Centerville who've been waiting by the border. And at their lead, walking most of the way is one person with one focus, one aim, one objective: the condition of those inside the craft. That person is Dr. Eugene Ritter.[9]

Dr. Ritter takes command. His first order is to Iowa's National Guard. "String a rope thirty yards away from the aircraft as a barrier inside which the medics, the ambulances, and rescue trucks can work."[36]

Charlie DePuy, Leo Craver, and searcher Milton Kruzich, who have each arrived on their separate paths, are watching the scene. Vehicles are moving into position, training their headlights into the open rear section created by the missing tail, lighting the path for Dr. Ritter. They see around him straps, thousands of wires, yellow oxygen masks hanging free, loose, unengaged, and something red/pink covering surfaces. Al Clark with the fire rescue truck views the passengers. They are strapped into their seats, their heads pitched forward, impacted with the seats in front. In the cockpit, the pilots are standing . . . overhead metal penetrates their heads . . . the one on the left, arm raised, fingers splayed. They are all immobile. Dr. Ritter is moving in silence, checking one victim and then the next. At his side is Iowa Highway Patrol Officer Sgt. James Douglas.[3, 9, 69]

The Crash Site
4:40 AM CT Wednesday

As Dr. Ritter works, and before sunrise, top investigators arrive at the crash site. The first, from Mountain View, California, his aircraft guided there by Byron Evans, is Najeeb Halaby, the head of the FAA. Second, from Denver, Colorado, are six top executives of Continental Airlines. Third, from Kansas City, are fifteen FBI agents with more following, including their supervisor, Mark Felt. The fourth, also from Kansas City, is Dewey Ballard the lead FAA Investigator for the Midwest and his team. This last team has walked following the trail of debris from Cincinnati, Iowa. They climb the crest of a hill. They see a crowd of police, medics, and bystanders surrounding the metal and bodies.[33, 36, 70]

Putnam County Sheriff Fowler is the fifth arrival. He sees a scene of catastrophe and in his jurisdiction. Before 5:00 AM, he's increasing his directives. The first is a distress message to Sgt. Herbert Nance at the 790th Radar Squadron in Sublette, Missouri. He asks for volunteers and equipment. Forty-four airmen immediately volunteer and are on their way in private vehicles for the forty-two-mile drive. A second message, another disaster message, is to Captain Thomas E. Bell, Acting Commander of the same squadron requesting reinforcements. Learning from the Continental officials the number of victims on board, thirty-seven passengers and a crew of eight—a total of forty-five—Sheriff Fowler orders George Choate, one of two editors of the *Unionville Republican* newspaper, to get Dr. Charles Judd, Unionville's doctor, to the scene. And he contacts more funeral directors from local communities: From Seymour (Liggett); from Unionville (Husted and Comstock); Kirksville (Riley); Lancaster (Norman); from Milan (Reggens). They are required to bring any extra vehicles to expand those already at the scene from Centerville: L.J. Johnson, Miller-Wehrle, the fire rescue truck and three station wagons from Hall Engineering. Sheriff Fowler places L.J. Johnson as the lead undertaker and orders distinguishing arm-bands for all funeral directors from Husted Funeral Home in Unionville, Missouri. [29, 44, 61, 71, 72]

Unionville, Missouri
5:00 AM CT Wednesday

George Choate is arriving at the home of Dr. Charles Judd. Dr. Judd assumes the news of an air crash is about a small aircraft. When he's told it's a big passenger jet, he knows "he has a huge problem." He grabs what he thinks he'll need and drives the six miles north. [12, 29, 74]

The Crash Site
5:05 AM CT Wednesday

Lead Undertaker L.J. Johnson is receiving explicit directions from authorities. No body is to be touched. Nothing is to be moved until an inspection team of FAA, FBI, and Continental Airlines is formed. It's a warning promptly reversed. One passenger is alive. [36, 44]

Inside Flight 11
5:06 AM CT Wednesday

As Dr. Ritter moves between the dead he hears a moan. It comes from half-way down on the right side of the fuselage. A young man is lying across three seats. He's briefly lucid. He gives his name: Takehiko Nakano. He asks for water. Dr. Ritter administers first-aid. There is no indication of external bleeding. His pulse is weak, rapid, "thready." Ritter calls for a stretcher. Assisting Dr. Ritter to extract Takehiko Nakano from the wreckage are two highway patrol officers, Iowa's Sgt. James Douglas, always at Dr. Ritter's side, and Missouri's Sgt. F.L. Staggs. Takehiko is placed in an ambulance driven by two members of the Centerville Fire Department, Gene Talbot and Larry Willis. They leave for Centerville's St. Joseph Mercy Hospital. "Call ahead and warn the hospital," says Ritter. "This man has survived a fall from 39,000 feet." The warning is relayed to Dr. Anthony Owca who leaves his home on Centerville's West Wall Street to receive the patient. Following the ambulance from the crash site, hoping Takehiko can give insight into the cause of the crash, is the Vice-President of Continental Airlines, John Kersey. [9, 12, 18, 28, 36, 75]

The Crash Site
5:30 AM CT Wednesday

As the ambulance carrying Takehiko Nakano leaves the crash site for Centerville, Dr. Charles Judd arrives from Unionville. There are no remaining aircraft survivors. He stands with Sheriff Fowler assessing the scene. Inside the fuselage Dr. Ritter continues his examination of the deceased. Alongside him members of the team of FAA, FBI, and Continental examiners take photographs of each body and write a description of its location inside the aircraft. At the front of the cabin where the craft hit the ground the hardest, the bodies are in disarray. Some lie tumbled over each other. There is dismemberment. Continental Airlines Secretary Paul K. Kreith phones FBI Director J. Edgar Hoover at the US Justice Department, Washington DC's Pennsylvania Avenue to request the formation of a disaster squad. This elite group of FBI agents are all highly trained forensic examiners. They are experts in fingerprint and latent (hidden) fingerprint analysis to aid the identity of Flight 11's victims. In response to Kreith's request, those agents begin assembling information in the twenty-one states—the home bases of all those on board.[3, 61, 72, 74]

In the main body of the aircraft where the impact was lighter, there is no dismemberment. All victims are in their seats. Groups of two or three men lift each body to remove it from the aircraft. One is twenty-eight-year-old Lieutenant Tom Thomas of the Centerville National Guard. The bodies he describes are thrust forward. They are immobile, slack, pliable. Each is lifted and handed to waiting funeral directors, the Centerville Fire Rescue Unit, the volunteers from Sublette's 790th Radar Squadron Station: Airmen Farley, Hicks, Mirick, and Grohs. Each body is then wrapped in plastic taken from 100 x 6 feet rolls delivered from Des Moines, and moved to waiting funeral cars. Sheriff David Fowler is supervising the process. So is Dr. Charles Judd. They have good reason.[61, 72, 74]

South Main Street, Centerville
5:40 AM CT Wednesday

A Centerville Fire Department ambulance driven by Larry Willis and Gene Talbot is arriving at Centerville's St. Joseph Hospital. It carries Takehiko Nakano, the only survivor of Continental Flight 11. Dr. Anthony Owca, the attending physician, is waiting with Registered Sister of Mercy Mary Owen. Takehiko is intermittently conscious. He is able to give his name. He asks for water. His pulse is high, his blood pressure low. An intravenous infusion is administered. He is made comfortable. His condition is perilous. [15, 18, 42, 65, 73, 77]

The Crash Site
5:50 AM CT Wednesday

It is at this point, as the bodies are about to be moved to the pre-pared National Guard morgue in Centerville, Iowa, that the relationship between the Missouri and Iowa authorities frays. The main fuselage of Flight 11, all bodies, and parts of bodies, are two-and-a-half miles south of the Iowa border. They are in Putnam County, Missouri. Putnam County's Coroner is Dr. Charles Judd and it is Dr. Judd who moves first. "If you cross the state line with those bodies, you're in big trouble." An argument ensues. It is heated. "We have a morgue ready. You don't. What would you do if we just took those bodies to Centerville?" Sheriff Fowler moves forward: "I'll shoot your tires out." With Putnam County prosecuting attorney absent from Putnam County, Dr. Judd appeals to the Attorney General of Missouri at his office in Jefferson City. Thomas Eagleton is thirty-two-years old, a rising star in the national Democratic Party. He's ten years away from his vice-presidential nomination and subsequent withdrawal on the George McGovern presidential ticket. Eagleton's response to Dr. Judd: the bodies stay in Missouri. A search for a building—a Missouri building—is now Judd's priority. He finds it on Unionville's West Main Street. The empty John Ryals Garage just east of the Methodist Church is quickly prepared by Unionville volunteers. The adjoining W.E. Ross building qualifies for suitable office space for incoming officials and journalists. They are already besieging the town with telephone calls.[11, 12, 74, 76]

Six miles northwest of Unionville, Missouri
6:00 AM CT Wednesday

A long dark night is ending. Daylight is suffusing, then yielding to streaming shafts of sunshine that lie in buttresses across the land. Weather forecasts promise a humid, sunny, hot day. It's still Leo Craver's "prettiest spring morning imaginable." But there on the Shuey land lies the broken remains of Continental Flight 11. The craft ripped, rough-cut into two, the entire tail section missing. Inside the cabin Dr. Eugene Ritter, a pipe clamped between his teeth, is still moving through the fuselage. Sgt. James Douglas is still at his side, so are FBI agents and Dewey Ballard the head of the FAA team from Kansas City. Their process is continuing: examining, photographing, recording locations, tagging the victims, removing them, wrapping them, placing them with the waiting morticians. All bodies are now being taken south to the morgue in Unionville's Ryals building.[9, 36, 78, 79, 81]

Surrounding the crash site there are ever-increasing numbers of law-enforcement personnel. Their voices are low. They are patrolmen, police, national guardsmen from Fairfield, and more from Centerville. National defense workers from Burlington, Iowa and sheriffs representing five Missouri counties are also on the scene (Adair, Gentry, Worth, Harrison, Mercer). From Iowa's Davis County is Jim Yates and from Wayne County, Louie Hart. Sheriff Hart and Iowa Patrol officer Howard Hays have walked cross-country south from Centerville Airport passing pieces of metal, suitcases, food trays, pillows. On seeing the wreck Sheriff Hart tells people back home in Corydon, "You would hardly know it had even been an airplane."[9, 11, 12, 72, 80, 87]

People have arrived through the night with specific wartime medical training. One is Ronnie Banks a US Army private, and another is Halga Jellison, a World War I survivor who brings his son Merlin from Powersville. Yet another is The Rev. Eldon Johnson, the Assistant Director of Admissions at William Jewell College in Liberty, Missouri. On Tuesday night he was giving a commencement address in Bethany, Missouri. When he heard the news, he drove straight to the crash site. Dr. Pat Gleason, who'd searched on foot with the Centerville volunteers through the night, brings his son Dan, a Centerville High School senior. Some hours previously they flew over the scene and could see the Centerville National Guardsmen already in place. Now the two are looking at the wreck on the ground and Dan wishes he'd stayed away. The scene he describes is "horrible:" Limbs of bodies . . . a severed head . . . sticking out of the ground like vegetables . . . imprints on the ground where the pilots, just before impact, had managed to get the front wheels down "for all the good it did". . . women identified only by their fingernail polish. 82, 83, 86, 88, 89

Kirksville, Missouri
6:15 AM CT Wednesday

On Kirksville's East Washington Street, Howard Watson is arriving at the Southwestern Bell office he manages. The breaking news, the emergency investigations, are throwing heavy loads on area telephone services. Operators are overwhelmed. They are dealing with calls from national media, from family members, from companies that had representatives on board. In Unionville, forty miles west, and in Milan, another eight miles beyond, the situation is desperate. Calls are being re-routed through Kirksville. And there's a further problem: At the crash site, Appanoose Sheriff Paul Thomas has told Sheriff David Fowler there are seven bodies in an almost straight line from the aircraft. They lie in a northeasterly direction for some three-and-a-half miles. Two are in the trees that fringe the alfalfa hayfield.

Some are in depressions caused by their fall. Most are unclothed. Airmen from the Sublette Radar Station have been posted to guard each body and some form of communication is needed to aid recovery. In response Howard Watson sends a crew from Kirksville. They build a portable temporary tower unit for radio circuits with transmitters for both senders and receivers. Another crew of fourteen personnel are arriving from Kirksville to make private lines, local lines, lines for long-distance, and toll lines. These are to serve the two headquarters established by Continental Airlines: one in the Ross building next to the morgue in Unionville and one in an empty farmhouse close to the ruined aircraft at the crash site. Their work continues through the morning. The authorities anticipate the arrival of the team that will take top investigative priority: the Civil Aeronautics Board (CAB). This eight-member team is on its way from Washington, DC. It will lead the prime investigation into the cause of Continental Flight 11's crash. The team is requesting thirty men to assist their work.[61, 90]

6:30 AM CT Wednesday

With so many more arrivals, Sheriff Fowler meets with the three families that live close to the crash site: the Bunnells, the Cooks, and the Webbers. He warns them to be prepared. Their lives are about to be heavily disrupted.[13, 30]

St. Joseph Mercy Hospital, Centerville
6:45 AM CT Wednesday

Dr. Anthony Owca and Sister Mary Owen are at the bedside of Takehiko Nakano. Silently waiting some distance away is John Kersey Continental Airline's Vice-President. He's been waiting over an hour since Takehiko's admittance. Kersey is hopeful Takehiko can tell him what happened aboard Flight 11 to cause it to fall 7.3 miles from the sky. But Takehiko's condition is deteriorating. There have been brief rallies. There have been indistinct words: once "none whatsoever" is heard clearly in English. Most words are in Japanese. There is no interpreter. In response to John Kersey's question Takehiko's unconsciousness deepens. Dr. Owca attempts artificial respiration. He is assisted by Dr. E.A. Larsen. The deterioration continues. Sister Mary Owen fears for Takehiko's soul. She asks is he a Christian? Has he been baptized? Sister Mary believes Takehiko says "Yes" to the first and "No" to the second. She administers the Sacrament of Baptism. There are murmurs, perhaps more words in Japanese. There's a moan. Takehiko dies. It is 6:50 AM. His death certificate is prepared and signed by Dr. E.A. Larsen. The cause of death: "irreversible shock—due to trauma in airplane accident—due to hemorrhage and other injuries."[3, 73, 91, 93, 94, 95, 96, 97, 98, 99]

The Crash Site
7:00 AM CT Wednesday

It's the beginning of a work day. Charlie DePuy has to get to Centerville to prepare the day's edition of the newspaper. He has to write the greatest local news story ever to occur in Iowegianland. Appanoose County Sheriff Paul Thomas drives Charlie to where he'd parked his car. It's from the Sheriff that Charlie learns the news of Takehiko Nakano's death.[3]

7:05 AM CT Wednesday

One mile west of the crash site eleven-year-old Marilyn Cook is leaving for school. Her little dog Mitzi is home and safe. But Marilyn knows of the crash. She's heard there are bodies in the trees. Neighbors drive Marilyn up the hill to Fife Country School. They are stopped by Centerville National Guardsmen. There are questions. Then they proceed.[32, 100]

A yellow Unionville, Missouri, public school bus is making its rounds. It collects Marilyn's fifteen-year-old sister Marla and seventeen-year-old brother Ronnie. Ronnie is the boy who found Flight 11, and he had been up searching through the night. The bus drives north and then east on the rural gravel road that leads to Shields Gas Station and Highway 5. It passes the line of trees that fringe the edge of the alfalfa hayfield. Ronnie sees bodies. They are still there. Bodies hanging in the trees. On the bus, all is quiet. No one speaks.[31, 64]

On the corner of Highway 5 and the rural gravel road, three Johnson children—Roger aged eleven, Claudia aged nine, and Charla aged seven—are waiting for the same school bus. They live close to the Shields gas station where their father, Junior Johnson, saw the flash in the sky at 9:17 PM the previous night. They are unaware of the crash, of the disaster that has happened so close to their home. On their land in long grass just yards away from where they wait, a victim lies strapped into her airline seat. As the three Johnson children wait for the bus, Roger practices his cornet. He chooses random music. He plays, "Taps." The three Johnson children board the bus. It turns south on Highway 5 for the seven-mile drive to school in Unionville.[17]

Centerville, Iowa
7:00 AM CT Wednesday

Charlie DePuy is at the *Daily Iowegian* newspaper office on North Main Street. He is assembling the first page for that day's edition. He chooses two-inch size letters for the banner headline: "JET LINER CRASHES HERE, 45 ARE KILLED." Below it Charlie vertically divides the page. On the right he places a photograph he took—his first sight of the aircraft that morning as he reached the brow of the Shuey hill. On the left he places a sub-heading. "Lone Survivor Dies In Hospital." He begins: "At 6:50 AM today, while Dr. Anthony Owca was applying artificial respiration in an effort to extend his life, the sole survivor of a Continental jet plane crash a short distance southwest of Cincinnati, Iowa, last night, died. Between the hours of 9:15 PM Tuesday and 6:50 AM today the greatest tragedy in Iowe-gianland history occurred."[3, 42]

7:20 AM CT Wednesday

On Midway, one block east of the *Iowegian* office, Mildred Earhart is the operator at the Iowa State Telephone Corporation office. She is dealing with both incoming and outgoing calls. The demands for long-distance services are higher than she can process. She transfers some to Charlie.[42]

John Vaira, the local agent for the Rock Island Railroad, tells Charlie he is finding articles from Flight 11 along the Rock Island right of way three-and-a-half miles east of Centerville. Lee Wyldes, the section foreman, has found a loose-leaf cover from the plane apparently furnished to Continental Airlines by the *Saturday Evening Post*. Sheriff Jim Yates of Davis County is finding blood–stained metal, a man's white shirt soaked with blood, a woman's white gloves, blankets, pillows with blood stains and the covers off the backs of plane seats bearing the Continental crest. They have been found at Lake Wapello forty miles northeast of the wreckage. Jeanne Harrington who'd fallen to the floor at a loud noise at 9:17 PM last night and who lives seven miles west of Lake Wapello is finding airline food trays on her land. Roscoe Wales, a former Appanoose County Sheriff, has found a woman's coat on the Frank Stajcar farm near the Fairview Church at Udell, Iowa. And blankets bearing the Continental crest are being found on the Laurel Bryant farm also in the Fairview Church vicinity.

Charlie continues his writing: "A giant Continental Jetliner became disabled in the storm-torn sky apparently near Lake Wapello in Davis County . . . and then fluttered through the air like some giant wounded bird, scattered objects and debris for thirty miles or more. . ."[30, 51]

South of Centerville
7:30 AM CT Wednesday

The scattered objects and debris from Charlie's "wounded bird" are a major issue for people living south of Centerville. In the early morning they are looking out at a confetti of aircraft metal, debris, and utensils. Joan Ervin, living southwest of Cincinnati, thinks it must have rained airplane parts. There's not a person who isn't finding some part in their yard. Earlier Joan was up in the night holding her one month old baby daughter Sharon. She heard planes flying low and wondered why. Her neighbor Peggy Sorrell comes to her back door and tells her there's an air crash somewhere near. There are airplane seats in her field. She's afraid to go there for fear they contain bodies. They turn on the radio. A man is broadcasting from Cincinnati, Iowa.[101, 102]

8:00 AM CT Wednesday

The news is across the country, across the world. It's the morning headlines in Los Angeles, Chicago, and Kansas City. Former Centerville resident Paul Lamantia is reading it in the *Detroit News*. In San Antonio, Texas, representatives of radio station KONO, Texas News Services have converged on pharmacist Paul Beer who operates the Broadway Pharmacy in Alamo Heights. They know he's from Centerville and they want the "inside" scoop. In England, living with her husband on a US Air Force base, Marilyn Heckhart (formerly Lowe of Centerville) hears it on the *BBC News*. She reads the names Dr. Ritter and Curtis Green in the overseas edition of *Stars and Stripes*. And five-hundred miles south of Centerville in Hot Springs, Arkansas, Charlotte Beck picks up a morning newspaper. Her husband Robert is the publisher and editor of the *Daily Iowegian*. They read a small box on the front page. It's a notice that a plane is missing in the Centerville area. That is all. No details. "Here I was five-hundred-fifty miles away, and maybe the biggest

story of all time breaking right in my own front yard. I said to Charlotte . . . well, there's nothing I can do. Charlie DePuy really knows
the ropes and will turn in a bang-up job." They start packing and
leave for home.[21, 39, 102, 103, 104, 105]

The Crash Site
8:15 AM CT Wednesday

Mark Felt, ten years before he's known as "Deep Throat" in the
Watergate scandal, is flying over the crash site in a small single engine
aircraft. He is the head of the FBI unit in Kansas City. A telephone
call at 5:30 AM awakened him with the news of Continental Flight
11. At 7:33 AM he's on his way to Centerville. He looks down and
sees the "incredible impact" the plane made as it hit the ground. It
came down at a forty-five-degree angle. The whole front portion
exploded from the force. He sees thirty to forty cars parked at the
edge of the field and a crowd of one hundred or more behind rope
barriers. Felt's plane circles several times then heads to the air strip in
Centerville. As the pilot prepares to land, he remarks he has no
experience of landing on grass strips. Felt knows he is kidding, but it
does nothing to improve the mood. Fifteen minutes later he reaches
the crash site. He can see deputies removing mangled body parts. He
feels utter despair at such a great loss of life. He cannot eat.[107]

8:30 AM CT Wednesday

At the Shuey field where Mark Felt is arriving, Putnam County
Sheriff David Fowler is attempting the impossible: to control the
crash site. There are more people. More police. More highway
patrol officers. More airmen from Sublette. More volunteers. More
news reporters from radio and television stations, from Associated
Press and United Press International. People are arriving carrying
sandwiches and coffee from Putnam County Red Cross, from

Unionville's Methodist and Baptist churches, from Centerville's Pale Moon Restaurant. A large food canteen on wheels arrives from Centerville's Salvation Army with two more on their way from Des Moines. Volunteers and airmen are picking up aircraft trim tabs, an electrical control unit for de-icing the vertical stabilizers, a window frame, sections of three blood-splattered seats, a comic book cover, paper cups, paper plates with the remains of pork bones, and soda cans, some full and bulging, some ripped, some compressed. They are gathering them into piles at the corners of the hayfield and on area roads.[29]

The noise increases. Every form of vehicle is pressed into use by Continental Airlines, jeeps, planes, and helicopters are landing and taking off on surrounding hillsides, terrifying Terry Bunnell's thirty-three dairy cows.[29]

Inside the fuselage, the team of Dr. Ritter, the FAA and FBI investigators are continuing to process the victims. Gloves are (gratefully) provided to those lifting the bodies. Twenty-three-year-old Jerry Kauzlarich with Centerville's National Guard watches the detached professionalism of the FBI agents. They are eating ham sandwiches as they examine the bodies. The waiting morticians move each victim with "the utmost calm, dignity and respect" to the morgue in Unionville. Near the fuselage Ed Huston, Unionville's rural mail carrier, and Marvin Steele, Unionville's new postmaster, are sorting one-thousand pounds of US mail that was on board. They clean the surfaces of maggots and send the mail forward. Nearby in his clerical collar, his long black cassock swaying as he moves, a purple stole around his shoulders, Father Joseph Anthamatten walks the length of the fuselage. He's the chaplain of St. Joseph Mercy Hospital, Centerville. He's been invited to the scene by Continental Airlines VP John Kersey. Father Joe finds at the break of the tail section, bent and misshapen airline silverware, a twisted stainless-steel knife. He finds shattered rosaries, pieces of clothing, bits of human remains. He's joined by his fellow missionary the Rev. Francis Weiner. They kneel. They pray. They grant each remain conditional absolution.[72, 91, 96, 108, 109]

There's something else moving close to the fuselage and around everyone at the scene. It's a dog. A gray and black, beautiful, friendly, eager, disciplined young German Shepherd. A dog with a cut below his chin. "Whose dog is this?" Sheriff Fowler finally asks. The answer: no one knows.[66]

Cincinnati, Iowa
9:00 AM CT Wednesday

The people of Cincinnati are stunned at the sight of Continental Flight 11's debris all over their town. They are echoing Joan Ervin: "It must have rained aircraft parts in the night." They follow with: "What do we do with all of this?" Cincinnati Mayor John Atkinson opens the town hall as a temporary storehouse for parts until the proper authorities can be notified. The authorities are the FBI and the FAA. They issue directives for both Cincinnati and Centerville. All large metal pieces—take them to the back of the Appanoose County Jail on Centerville's North Main Street. Take smaller items to the Fire Station on Centerville's Highway 2. Accompany each item with your name, your address, and where the item was found.[110, 111]

One mile east of Cincinnati, Wayne Smothers sees clothes, possessions, and luggage littering his fields. FBI agents have roped off the area. No one is permitted access. It's less than a mile up the road to Gabe Raskie's wooded, undulating land. It's there Gabe finds a briefcase. A brown leather briefcase. It's near a fence line. It is wide open and empty. No papers lie near, and there are three letters on the front: TGD. Gabe delivers the briefcase to Centerville's fire station. Later, FBI agents collect it. One agent is heard to say, "This is what we've been looking for." Four FBI agents are knocking at the rural home of Gabe Raskie: "Show us where you found this briefcase."[5, 112, 113]

The Crash Site
9:00 AM CT Wednesday

Dr. Charles Judd and Lester Cook are in an army helicopter. They are traveling the three-and-a-half mile line northeast from the impact site. They find seven bodies that have fallen from Flight 11's tail section. Just east of Cleo and Ila Jean Webber's barn they find the body of the young soldier who was returning to Ft. Riley, Kansas. He is still strapped into his seat. Dr. Judd examines him and believes he might have been alive when he hit the ground. Hanging in the tree line they find the body of a man. His intestines are exposed. An identifying bracelet gives a name: Doty. They continue the search over this rough hilly land. It's a long process. At each location Dr. Judd is seeing "an elderly lady with a cane and a young woman with a baby." "Every time the 'copter [spots] one of the seven bodies and sets down by it, these two ladies were there." They seem to be everywhere. Dr. Judd suggests to the pilot to just follow them— "they are making better time than us."[5, 12, 74, 114, 115]

Near the Shields Gas Station
10:00 AM CT Wednesday

Junior Johnson is returning home. He has delivered a tractor to a farm in southern Iowa. His three children are at school in Unionville. Junior sees black cars traveling at high speeds. He notes how smooth they've made the surface of the gravel road that comes from the west to meet Highway 5 at the Shields gas station. He sees an army helicopter descend to his land close to his house. It lifts a victim from the long grass. She's still strapped into her seat.[17]

Highway 65 North of Hot Springs, Arkansas
11:00 AM CT Wednesday

Robert Beck, the publisher and editor of *The Centerville Daily Iowegian* and his wife Charlotte are on their way home. They are listening to the 11:00 AM *NBC News* with Chet Huntley reporting. Huntley says, "And now we'll take you to Centerville, Iowa, for a report on the Continental Airlines wreck . . ."[90]

Two-hundred-thirty miles north and traveling north on the same highway is the Unionville, Missouri, school's senior class. They have just spent their senior trip at Rockaway Beach in Missouri's Ozarks and are returning home. They hear the news of the crash of Continental Flight 11 on the school bus radio. The reaction is silence. In 1962 in rural Missouri, little is known of passenger jet aircraft. But this they know: the news is serious. It is eventful. It is life-altering.[116]

Unionville, Missouri
11:30 AM CT

At the morgue on West Main Street eight area funeral morticians are awaiting instructions. They come with George Coffey, Continental Airline's Assistant Public Relations Officer. He reads the list of the victims. He pauses at each name. He cites where each body must be transported. He gives religious requirements: two of the victims are of the Jewish faith. They will not be embalmed. They will be wrapped in a simple white shroud and there will be no coffin.[44, 117]

Continental's D. Claybourne makes two telephone calls. The first is to the Batesville Casket Company in Batesville, Indiana. He requests forty-three identical Monosealer caskets. They are to leave the company's factory by 9:00 AM tomorrow—Thursday, May 24—to start the fifteen-hour drive by truck to Unionville. Mr. Claybourne's second call is to Cordell White at the Frigid Fluid Company of Chicago. He requests forty-five disaster pouches, one for each victim. Mr. White responds that he will personally conduct them by express train to La Plata, Missouri, and deliver them to Unionville. They will arrive today at midnight.[36, 44]

The leader at the morgue in charge of the bodies is Mark Felt, the head of the FBI in Kansas City. The funeral directors follow his instructions. They divide the morgue into three sections. They are labeled: "Airline," "FBI," and "Autopsy." Unionville's Police Department diverts traffic from West Main Street. The bodies of the victims arrive unimpeded. So do flowers, wreaths, and garlands sent by relatives and the community. Thirty bodies have already arrived. This includes Takehiko Nakano brought by Al Clark from Centerville's St. Joseph Mercy Hospital. Al's partner is Paul Hindley. L.J. Johnson the lead mortician is carefully monitoring all those involved with the bodies. He sees the physical and emotional toll that is being exacted.[36, 37, 44, 118]

The Crash Site
Noon CT Wednesday

A helicopter is landing on a field near the fuselage. It brings eight members of the Accident Investigation Team of the Civil Aeronautics Board (CAB). This is the A Team. Their investigations will determine the cause of Continental Flight 11's crash. Their report will be presented to Congress and to the American people. The team's leader is George A. Van Epps. At forty-years of age, he is the nation's top expert on Boeing 707s. His career has covered previous 707 accidents. Second in command is fifty-one-year-old Edward E. Slattery Jr., the board's communication director. With them are six experts on every phase of a Boeing 707's functions.[119, 120]

They are met by the other investigative teams: from the FBI, the FAA, and Continental Airlines. Together they circle the fuselage. They record their observations. The aircraft on impact was facing west. The nose is dug into the ground at a twenty-degree angle on a ten-degree slope of the alfalfa hay field. The thirty-eight-foot tail section is missing. So are twenty-nine feet of the left wing and all four engines. There is telescoping behind the cockpit but the remaining fuselage, though broken, is intact. In the cabin, Captain Gray, First Officer Edward Sullivan, and Second Officer Roger Allen are in their normal crew locations. They are wearing smoke masks. The face plates are demolished; blood and tissue adhere. Oxygen hoses are broken. The landing gear is down and locked. Between the Captain's yoke and the aircraft instrument panel there is an emergency check list. On the same panel two clocks have stopped. One reads 21.21:15 PM, the other 21.21:45 PM.[1, 39]

Najeeb Halaby, the head of the FAA, is "terribly shaken." He is upset at the condition of Captain Gray, of the crew, of the whole tragic scene of human tragedy, of the destruction of such a beautiful aircraft. He was the first high official to arrive. He's flown through the night from Mountain View, California. He hasn't slept. He wants to hold a press conference. "What the hell for?" asks Don Wilson the ranking Continental Airlines official and Vice-President for flight. Halaby addresses the press and, aware the aircraft had traveled through a storm, says, "This is what happens when you fly through thunderstorms." Both Van Epps and Slattery remain mute. But Don Wilson is furious. Halaby's words are a reflection on Continental's favorite and loved pilot. "You'll rue the day you ever said that."[2, 35]

The Crash Site
1:00 PM CT Wednesday

By 1:00 PM at the crash site, order is disintegrating. The three families—the Cooks, the Bunnells, and the Webbers—are being besieged. Reporters from newspapers, radio, and television stations are rushing to their homes to use their telephones. And their bathrooms. They use the telephones to communicate their accounts to their editors. Terry Bunnell finds a line of them waiting in his living room with one reporter shoving himself to the front of the line. Some reporters are courteous. Others are tactless. They insult local people. Ila Jean Webber hears one from New York City talking to his New York editor and saying, "I want you to know that I'm calling from bush country." Some color their reports with inaccuracies. And one in the Cook home appears startled there is only one TV channel . . . and he tells Marilyn he's missing Dr. Kildare. Another describes the grass runway at Centerville Airport to Gene Horn: "You could roll it up and put it in your pocket." For Dr. Judd the media people are driving him "nuts." They are hounding him everywhere. Once he is interviewed by Pauline Frederick, the pioneer woman journalist at NBC, ". . . by telephone during a live television evening news program, and I didn't even know." But nothing prepares them or the authorities for what is next. They call it pandemonium.[12, 43, 74, 114, 121]

With the news across the country, people are arriving in tidal waves. For miles along Highway 5 they are double-parked, restricting necessary traffic. These are not the helpers . . . not the investigators . . . not the news people. These are the curious. The people drawn to accidents. The people compelled to sights of human tragedy. And some are morbid voyeurs. Some are hurtling along country lanes. Some are driving across open fields and getting stuck. Some are walking miles from no one knows where and collapse in the heat. They are leaving farm gates open. They are cutting fences. One steals Terry Bunnell's tractor and burns out the radiator. They are trampling the eight-acre cornfield that was just emerging from the ground. And there are new roads through the oat field near the entrance to Terry Bunnell's farm. Sheriff Fowler gets permission to close Highway 5. He uses public speaking equipment borrowed from the Paul Turner store in Centerville. It makes little difference. And then there are the macabre—those with perverted curiosity who are finding ways to get close to the bodies—to get souvenirs, to steal from their pockets. It's Dr. Ritter who takes care of that lot. He emerges from the fuselage and tells them what he thinks of them. He uses military phrases and military words. "He is mean," says Gene Horn. ". . . Sergeant Major mean. And we are glad of it."[5, 13, 29, 60]

1:50 PM CT Wednesday

And everywhere there's a dog. The same beautiful, friendly young German shepherd with a cut below his muzzle. Sheriff Fowler turns to his brother Bob who is a deputy sheriff assisting him. "Do you think your boy Robert would come for this dog before someone claims him?" And that is how seven-year-old Robert Fowler acquires the dog. A dog who could perform every trick in the book— a dog who broke through a glass window the night of a severe storm. A dog that was never claimed. A dog Robert named Boeing 707. [66, 67]

Springfield, Missouri
2:00 PM CT Wednesday

Bob Beck—the publisher and editor of the *Centerville Daily Iowegian*—and his wife Charlotte are making good time. They have crossed the border from Arkansas into Missouri and have reached Springfield. All the way they have listened to a steady news flow: CBS, NBC, the noon news reports. The crash of Flight 11 is the top story of the day. In Springfield it's the banner headline of the newspaper, *The Springfield Leader and Press*: "Airliner Rips Apart in Flight, With Death for all 45 Aboard." There's a subheading: "Big Jet Found in North Missouri Pasture." Bob Beck waits fifteen minutes. He knows the press rush time for the *Centerville Daily Iowegian* will have subsided. He calls Charlie DePuy. It's Gladys who answers. Charlie has been up all night following the story. Gladys says, "It is the biggest story ever to hit Centerville." Bob agrees. He and Charlotte drive on north on Highway 65. [34, 90, 104]

Unionville, Missouri
2:15 PM CT Wednesday

Dr. Charles Judd, his helicopter search for seven bodies completed, arrives at the morgue. He's immediately under pressure. He's the coroner for Putnam County. He's in command of all bodies second only to FBI Director Mark Felt. A message has been received from the Central Intelligence Committee—autopsies are to be carried out on all forty-five bodies. Dr. Judd knows the law: a coroner can be liable if an autopsy is performed without the consent of the nearest relative . . . but forty-five such consents? He makes his second call to Jefferson City, to Missouri Attorney General Thomas Eagleton. "Call a Coroner's Jury" says Eagleton, "one inquest will be held. Perform autopsies on each case where the Coroner's Jury demands it." Dr. Judd appoints six Putnam County citizens to form his jury. They are Don Shuey, Bill Davis, Leonard Rouse, Henry Gardner, George Brundage, and Ralph Roof. They view the bodies. They consider the known facts. They return their verdict: "The deceased came to their death by an unknown cause."[12, 29, 74, 114]

Centerville, Iowa
2:30 PM CT Wednesday

At the *Daily Iowegian* office on North Main Street, Charlie DePuy has completed writing that day's edition of the newspaper. Louis Ver Baere is doing the engraving and "really applying the steam" to the printing press, anticipating a demand for extra copies. Throughout the morning there are rumors about the cause of the crash—that it was the result of a collision with another aircraft. Jack Donovan, a Des Moines based Associated Press (AP) reporter tells Charlie at the *Iowegian* of a light plane—a Cessna 180 or 182—that left Fairfield Airport and never returned. Dean Gabbert of the *Fairfield Ledger* reports there was only one Cessna at Fairfield Airport and that's accounted for. The rumors continue until J.M. Newman the Associate Administrator for the FAA Central Region says he's read the radar reading. There was only ONE "blip" in the vicinity. And that was Continental Flight 11. No other "blips."[3]

More phone calls bring reports to Charlie of Flight 11 debris far from the point of impact—all to the northeast. The back of a seat, napkins, insulation near Ottumwa sixty miles away; a Flight 11 hostess log book, foam rubber, paper napkins one-hundred-eighty miles away at Mechanicsville; a cancelled check signed by hostess Joyce

Rush at Madison, Wisconsin over three-hundred miles to the northeast. The next predominant rumor is the crash was the result of a thunderstorm.[121, 123]

The Morgue in Unionville, Missouri
2:45 PM CT Wednesday

In the "airline" section of the morgue the funeral directors are receiving each body. All clothing is removed. The clothes and all contents are saved and put into separate containers. Each container is given a number—the same number given to the victim at the crash site.

One by one the bodies are then moved to the "FBI" area for identification. The details of each victim are recorded: height, weight, eye and hair color, any distinguishing mark—a scar, a bent finger, an aberration, a deformity. And each is fingerprinted. This coincides with the arrival from Washington DC of the Disaster Squad, the elite FBI team trained in forensics, fingerprints, and latent (hidden) identification. They arrive with evidence from twenty-seven states, from military, government, job application records and dental records. They have also collected latent fingerprints from four states. These include prints from a bottle of perfume, a car window, desk accessories, and personal items.[44, 74, 114, 124]

Centerville, Iowa
3:00 PM CT Wednesday

Robert Webb, the president of Centerville Chamber of Commerce, and Boyd O'Briant, the executive secretary, are on the phone with their equivalents in Unionville, Missouri. Where will all these people spend the night? In Centerville, the FBI has reserved Motel 60 for thirty of their agents. Hotel Continental, which has been appointed as the Civil Aeronautics Board's Official Headquarters, has had rooms reserved for all the CAB team. In Unionville, with a quarter of Centerville's population, accommodations for several hundred have been found and one-hundred-fifty cots are set up in the Methodist and Christian Churches. Every private home has offered to take guests. [123, 124, 125]

The Crash Site
3:30 PM CT Wednesday

The first focus of Van Epps, Slattery of the CAB, and all the investigators is the aircraft's flight recorder. This will have recorded Flight 11's speed, altitude, compass heading, gravity forces, and time sequence to the moment of impact. They find it in the wheel well. It's the size of a basketball. It's in good condition. It's wrapped in cotton and dispatched by a special courier to Washington DC. There a detailed and precise laboratory analysis will be made. The results could take days. [82, 93, 124, 126]

The investigators issue a joint conclusion. Continental Flight 11 broke apart in the air and while in flight, not on impact. To find the cause is their next focus. They examine pieces of the fuselage. They lift them. They examine each, closely turning them, noting marks and scratches and smudges. They smell them. They examine the wing, the fuel tank found four miles to the northeast and the septic facility under the toilets of the aircraft. They bring in Bob Buss of Centerville's Hall Engineering Company to record the location of each discovery. And they note the vital pieces of the craft that are missing. Searches for these continue—chief among them, the aircraft's thirty-eight-foot missing tail section. It could be underwater. Appanoose County Sheriff Paul Thomas calls on his posse trained in scuba searches. Leo Craver, who had found the first piece of metal on Highway 5, the first indicator of this tragedy, prepares himself. In his regulation, full over-the-head bodysuit, attached flippers and yellow oxygen tank, he descends into the ponds, lakes, and rivers of the area. His assignment: find missing aircraft pieces. Leo finds nothing. [91, 119, 123, 127, 129, 130, 131]

Southwest of the Shuey Field
4:00 PM CT Wednesday

In the air southwest of the wreckage, Lester Cook is flying with an army helicopter pilot. Lester is the area's authority on this land with its hills and valleys and woods. He and the pilot are searching for Continental Flight 11's four Pratt and Whitney JT3C-6 engines. When the tail separated from the aircraft the remaining structure pitched nose-down violently causing the engines to tear off and follow their own trajectories. Lester finds them—each fifteen-feet long—slammed into the ground at different locations all southwest of the main wreckage on the farmland of Bill Bernecker.[5, 132]

The Crash Site
5:00 PM CT Wednesday

The eight CAB investigators work in couples, in groups, and sometimes alone. George Van Epps and Edward Slattery—good friends who've worked together at other 707 disasters—frequently work together. When their frustration is high, the two sing hymns. Loudly. Slattery never hits a true note. But it releases their tension. All eight CAB members are forming theories. The first—an in-air collision. It is already ruled out by J.M. Newman, Assistant Administrator for the FAA Central Region who'd phoned Charlie DePuy to say he'd read the radar reading and there was only one "blip." With more theories the investigators discuss each one together in debate format. One investigator proposes a theory. The others examine, question, and challenge it. Then the next theory: air turbulence is prominent in their discussions. The investigators acquire the recordings of the conversation between Captain Fred Gray, his crew, and the Waverly Radar Control Operator. John M. Beardsley at the FAA Central Region says, "The conversation indicated the plane got through the squall line . . ." A third theory is "Clear Air Turbulence." This comes like a tidal wave frequently on the back side of a squall line when there's not a cloud in the sky. Then there's the possibility of engine malfunction and an explosion on board. Van Epps calls in more experts from around the country.[61, 128, 133]

Southwest Appanoose County
6:00 PM CT Wednesday

The Centerville Fire Rescue Team members have been without sleep for twenty hours. They return to where Gene Horn found the wing and the fuel tank. They follow the trail southwest, pushing through the undergrowth, wading through the mud.[43]

Centerville Airport
6:30 PM CT Wednesday

A DC3 is landing at the Centerville Airport. It brings from Kansas City Robert "Bob" Six, the CEO of Continental Airlines. He's been enroute for twelve hours from Paris to New York to Kansas City and now Centerville. Normally forceful and energetic, Six is weary, red-eyed, and badly shaken. He's met by Don Wilson Continental Vice-President for Flight. Together they drive to the crash site. On the way Six asks, "Which 707?" "7-5," says Wilson . . . "Yeah, the same one that was hi-jacked at El Paso." At the Shuey field, Six looks at the wreckage. "What could we have done to prevent this?" He wants to go to the morgue to view the bodies. Wilson talks him out of it. Wilson and Six stay up most of the night drinking coffee at the Pat Gleason home in Lane Heights where Six will stay. They recall Captain Fred Gray. He was a close friend to both. Six remembers how Fred never attended a recurrent training class without wearing his twin trademarks, white shoes and a red carnation.[86, 90, 137]

Unionville, Missouri: The Morgue
6:45 PM CT Wednesday

In the "FBI" section of the morgue, establishing the identity of the first thirty-nine bodies is routine. For the next five, the identities are challenging. The five are mutilated. Two of them are dismembered. Identifying these five becomes the concentrated work of the FBI Disaster Squad working together with Dr. Judd. The Squad offers pointers: names on clothes, items in pockets, an appendectomy scar on one of the hostesses. The FBI announces, "The FBI in no manner certifies as to the finality of these identifications. They are being prepared for the assistance of the proper authorities. It shall be the final decision of the Putnam County, Missouri, authorities as to whether sufficient data has been developed for the purpose of establishing the identification of each of these victims." In other words the identity of all five will be the ultimate judgment of the forty-four-year-old Coroner of Putnam County, Dr. Charles Judd. Dr. Judd calls for help from Putnam County's dentist, Dr. R.H. McCalment, to assist him. McCalment identifies fillings, extracted teeth, and gold crowns and compares them with dental records of the victims from their dentists in New York, Wisconsin, Chicago, and Santa Monica, California.

Bodies of Continental Flight 11's crew and two passengers are moving into the "Autopsy" section of the morgue. At the same time, the number of the bodies is being tallied. Thirty-nine plus five equals forty-four. One body is missing.[44, 82]

5 miles north of the Crash Site
7:00 PM CT Wednesday

It is in the evening light they find it—the empennage, the tail section with its fin and rudder. There among the trees in Section 13 of Franklin Township in Iowa's Appanoose County. Five-hundred pieces lying perfectly flat, their metal skin curled, pushed right out over rivet heads, surrounded by fragments of aircraft interior. It's Centerville's Fire Department's team that finds the pieces and brings the CAB, the FAA, and Continental investigators to the site. They look closely at the bulges, the deformations of the aircraft skin pushed straight out. It was evidence of a tremendous explosive force. It was one of Dewey Ballard's team from Kansas City who lifts one piece, smells a distinctive odor, a distinct smoke. He looks at the others and says, "Fireworks." FBI Director Mark Felt is informed.[28, 43]

Unionville, Missouri
8:00 PM CT Wednesday

At the morgue on West Main Street, thirty bodies, their identities assured, are released from the "FBI" section to the funeral directors. Embalming begins at 8:00 PM, the two victims of the Jewish faith exempted. The directors are working with two morgue tables, four pressure machines, seven or eight men at a time. Agricultural stock tanks are brought into the basement of the building. They are filled with ice. They hold the completed bodies. Dr. Judd remains in the "FBI" section until midnight continuing his identification of five of the bodies. The crew of seven and two passengers are still in the "autopsy" section. One body remains missing. Mark Felt leaves to meet with CAB's George Van Epps and Edward Slattery at the Centerville Continental Hotel. They will discuss the nature of the explosion in the tail section and the powder burns found on two hostesses and "explosive residue" on one passenger revealed in the FBI examinations. Reporters in Centerville approach Mark Felt: "Are there indications that any unnatural factors could be involved in the crash?" His reply: "No comment."[44, 134, 135, 136]

The Crash Site
9:00 PM CT Wednesday

Two sheriffs, Appanoose County's Paul Thomas and Putnam County's David Fowler, are in discussion. They are planning their search for the missing victim of Flight 11 the next day. Paul Thomas, his posse, and volunteers will start at the crash site, follow the trail of the debris northeast, and continue for the forty miles if necessary to Lake Wapello in Davis County. David Fowler's plan is to assemble searchers from the Kirksville National Guard, Unionville, and area high school seniors, juniors, and sophomores should they wish to take part. His plan is a circular one—to start at Shields Gas Station on Highway 5, walk eight miles west of the area and eight miles back if the body is not located. [18, 71, 82, 91, 93, 138, 139, 140, 141]

Unionville, Missouri
Midnight CT Wednesday

It's been a long drive from Hot Springs, Arkansas. Bob Beck, the publisher and editor of the *Centerville Daily Iowegian* and his wife Charlotte have reached Unionville and stop at Ray Fowler's food stand. It's directly across the street from the morgue. "It's a terrible accident," Ray Fowler tells Bob and Charlotte. "As long as people are working there—I will stay open all night." [90]

Inside the morgue the funeral directors are still working. Cordell White of Frigid Fluid has kept his word. He has personally brought forty-five disaster pouches by express train from Chicago to LaPlata, Missouri, and driven them north to Unionville. Assisting him, driving in a station wagon from Centerville, is Homer Sweet. With him is his son, thirteen-year-old Rick. The pouches are heavy rubber bags with tight zipper closures. Each body—those that have been embalmed—has an identity tag tied to a left toe and is placed in one of these pouches. Six airmen from Sublette guard the bodies for the night. [39, 44, 139]

Thursday, May 24, 1962

The Crash Site
5:47 AM CT Thursday

The first light . . . Sunrise . . . Thursday, May 24—the second day. Key CAB, FAA, FBI, and Continental Airlines investigators, their night spent in Unionville, Centerville, and Kirksville, are moving to two points of convergence—the fuselage on the Shuey Field, and five miles north across the Iowa State line, lying between the trees, the five-hundred pieces of Continental Flight 11's tail section.[138]

Today, security is tight. E.W. Fannon, the former Superintendent of Centerville Schools, now writing articles for the *Daily Iowegian,* describes a "tight military ring" around the whole area, limiting access to Continental Airline officials and the FBI. Visitors are required to show credentials. Fannon obliges. He's then escorted to the Terry Bunnell home for a prearranged interview with the family. He's escorted by Gene Crawford, Terry Bunnell's brother-in-law, who is a service member of the Centerville National Guard Company B Heavy Tank Division. Both the airmen from Sublette and Center-ville National Guard are patrolling and protecting the crash sites. In addition, Missouri Governor John Dalton orders the National Guard in Kirksville to mobilize and report to Putnam County Sheriff, David Fowler, at the crash site. Fifty-two guardsmen are scrambling to prepare their heavy guns and small cannons capable of firing mis-siles in high trajectories.[13, 91, 140]

Unionville, Missouri
8 AM CT Thursday

Three procedures are underway at the morgue in the Ryals Garage building on West Main Street. US Army pathologists, ruling out a heart attack or carbon monoxide poisoning that could have led to the crash, continue performing autopsies on the crew members of Continental Flight 11. When all bodies have been examined, toxicological and pathological samples are gathered and refrigerated. They are flown for analysis to the Armed Forces Institute of Pathology on the grounds of the Walter Reed Army Medical Center in Washington DC. The results will not be known for some time.[141]

L.J. Johnson and seven other area morticians are embalming the remaining bodies. They receive the bodies one at a time after autopsy and identification. And as they did the night before, the victim's identity is written on a label and tied to the left toe. The body is then placed in a disaster pouch and surrounded by ice in the basement. By 9:00 AM the morticians are told trucks carrying forty-three caskets have begun their fifteen-hour drive from Batesville, Indiana, to Unionville.

Dr. Charles Judd is working with Unionville's dentist, Dr. R.H. McCalment and US Army pathologists. By a process of elimination, they are identifying six of the victims. This same process reveals something of the missing body. She is one of the flight hostesses.[44, 74, 136]

Centerville
9:00 AM CT Thursday

At the *Daily Iowegian* offices on North Main Street south of the Centerville Square, the telephone is ringing. Charlie DePuy who has managed to acquire some sleep, answers. The voice, a man's, is calling from New York City. Charlie hears distress in the voice. "Can you tell me if Sidney H. Goldberg has been positively identified as one of the passengers of the Continental plane that crashed near

Centerville?" Charlie checks. "He is officially listed on the passenger list." "But," insists the voice from New York, "Has he been identified beyond any doubt?" Charlie responds, "There are six bodies not yet identified. Every possible means is occurring to provide a name for each." Charlie is sensing the urgency of the man who is calling. He's grasping at straws hoping something, somehow might have kept Sidney Goldberg off the flight.[82, 142]

Across Centerville Square at the Milani Law Office another phone is ringing. Sixty-two-year-old George Milani answers. The speaker is Kansas City lawyer Morton Rosenberg a fellow University of Iowa Law School graduate with Jim Milani, George's twenty-nine-year-old son and law partner. This too is emotional. Morton Rosenberg's good friend Marcus Brand, an administrator in Kansas City's Brand and Pirowitz Coat and Suit Company, is a victim of Flight 11. Morton's request is that Jim and his father facilitate the speedy departure of Marcus Brand's body from the morgue for burial in Kansas City.[143, 145]

George and Jim drive to the morgue. Marcus Brand and Sidney Goldberg, both victims of Flight 11, are of the Jewish faith and, following Jewish custom, the dead must be buried swiftly. Two Kansas City funeral cars, hired by the Brand and Goldberg families, are already waiting at the door of the morgue. The Milanis—George and Jim—assist Dr. Judd and the funeral directors. The bodies depart for Kansas City.[143, 144]

The Putnam/Appanoose Border Land
10:00 AM CT Thursday

Robert "Bob" Beck, the publisher and editor of the *Centerville Daily Iowegian*, home from Hot Springs, Arkansas, has given himself an assignment. He is touring and recording the "pulse" of the people of the area—their reaction to the tragedy that is around them. He starts in Unionville, Missouri, "the nerve center of activity."[146]

C. Eldon Dickson working in the Herrick Drug Store uses two words: "Deep shock." Don Herrick, the drug store's owner is drinking a cup of coffee at a nearby restaurant. "Everyone feels the gravity of the accident." Ray Fowler runs the Dairy Lane across from the morgue. Bob Beck talked to him when he drove north from Hot Springs the previous night. Today Ray Fowler tells Bob, "It's like a lot of things. You read about it in the paper and you don't think much about it. But when you see something like this, you can appreciate the great tragedy involved." Standing close by, Perry W. Porter, the Putnam County land surveyor agrees. "It just couldn't be a worse tragedy." From local attorney Clair Magee, "People just want to be helpful. The community has opened its heart in every way possible standing by ready to do whatever is asked."[146]

Charles Smith, a Unionville policeman, and Joe Bacon, a Missouri highway patrolman, tell Bob that nine extra Missouri patrolmen have been on duty in Unionville but, unlike the crowd at the crash site, the crowd in Unionville has been orderly. It is Dr. Judd at the morgue who reports one incident. A man with a camera twice attempted to take photographs of the dead. He was physically thrown out by the "collar and britches" by the FBI Chief Mark Felt while "Doc" as everyone calls Dr. Judd in Unionville, held the door open. The doctor and Felt enjoy a mutually respectful relationship. Mark Felt consults Dr. Judd at every event. "Is this OK with you Coroner?" "Can we go ahead with this Coroner?"[5, 146]

Next door to the morgue in the W.E. Ross Building, Continental Airlines has set up its headquarters. George Coffey, the airline's Assistant Director for Public Relations is regularly in contact with Mark Felt, the FBI agents, the doctors, the morticians in the front part of the morgue. He is also always available to the press. This morning they are visited by Robert Six, the president of Continental Airlines, who has spent the night with the Gleason family in Centerville after arriving from Paris. Robert tells Bob Beck, "The people of Unionville have been most understanding and sympathetic. I extend my sincere thanks to everyone concerned." Don Wilson, the vice president for flight adds, "I wish to thank all of them on behalf of Continental Airlines."[146]

There is another incident. It's unseen and unknown. Two small boys look into the morgue from an open door at the far end. They see bodies lying in body bags. And there's a hand. A white, still hand extending just beyond the bag zipper. And on a finger is a diamond. One large and brilliant diamond.[66]

The Crash Site
11:00 AM CT Thursday

The army of extra experts petitioned by George Van Epps, the head of the CAB, is arriving. They come in small aircraft to Centerville Airport, by transportation vehicles, cars, jeeps, and helicopters landing at the site. They represent every aspect, every component, every mechanical detail of a 707 jet airliner, and they work without delay.[142]

The Pratt and Whitney engine experts are guided by Lester Cook to the Bill Bernecker Farm. All four engines of Continental Flight 11 are at separate locations in an area a half-mile wide and three-quarters of a mile long. The engine closest to the main fuselage lies one-and-one-eighth of a mile to the southwest. All four engines are buried in the ground. Unionville contractor Lavan Smith brings his mechanical digger to extract them. He's finding it no easy task . . . given the trajectory at which they'd buried themselves. The experts' subsequent examination reveals "little or no rotation of compressors or turbines at ground impact."[1, 142, 148]

The Severe Storm Unit of the US Weather Bureau arrives from Kansas City. Its members start with an appeal to all residents within a fifty-mile radius of the crash scene. They want any knowledge of violent weather on Tuesday, May 22—funnel clouds, large hail, damaging winds. They make a special appeal to anyone who might have a recording barograph to contact them.[16, 128]

But for most of the investigators, the specialists in hydraulics, wiring, fuel, Boeing jet structures, the engineers and the metal experts, the key location, the one receiving the closest scrutiny is the tail section. The empennage with the fin and the rudder is lying in five-hundred large pieces. Thousands more tiny fragments lie between the trees five miles northeast of the fuselage in Section 17 of Franklin Township, Appanoose County.[138, 141]

Shields Gas Station
12:30 PM CT Thursday

The search for the missing body begins at Shields gas station on Highway 5. Forty hours earlier on Tuesday night, Junior Johnson was locking the station for the night and saw a brilliant flash that lit the sky. Today hundreds of people are assembling here to search for the missing victim of Continental Flight 11 . . . one of its crew, a stewardess. "We will search the full flight line in Iowa," Appanoose County Sheriff Paul Thomas tells Charlie DePuy, "And Sheriff Fowler is organizing a similar search to take place in Missouri." Facing the forty-mile flight line in Iowa, the hundreds of Iowa volunteers leave at 12:30 PM. They are walking north and east.

The two-hundred-fifty Missouri volunteers follow a plan laid out by George Choate one of the editors of the *Unionville Republican*. They will leave Shields gas station, walk an eight-mile path, then turn around and make another trip if the body is not found. Volunteers ready for the search are Unionville and other Missouri high school seniors, juniors, and sophomores, all boys. They are joined by the Bethany High School football team, peace officers, members of Continental Airlines and the Kirksville unit of the National Guard. They begin their eight-mile path to the southwest. They are led by Putnam County Sheriff David Fowler and Sheriff Clay Delemeter of Mercer County. They all are walking side by side. Some are holding hands.[17, 138]

The Crash Site
3:15 PM CT Thursday

Battery B, 2nd Howitzer Battalion and the 128th Field Artillery are arriving from Kirksville. It was Missouri's Governor Dalton who mobilized these groups, ordering them to report to the crash site. There are fifty-two of them under the command of Captain Colin Campbell and Lt. Duane Norman. They arrive at 3:15 PM to relieve the Centerville National Guard that has been on duty for thirty-six hours. The Kirksville replacements move into the campground area on the Shuey land one-hundred yards from the main wreckage. They form themselves into seven two-man posts and are placed on a twenty-four-hour guard rotation. [138, 143]

Two miles east of the Crash Site
3:25 PM CT Thursday

It's 3:25 PM. The last victim of Continental Flight 11 is found. She lies in knee high grass east of a pond on a tree-lined slope close to Highway 5 in what is known as Kozad Park. This is Cleo Webber's land. The body is just a few hundred yards from the Webber home and not far from where the other five victims who had fallen from the tail section. She's found by Marvin McKinney, a volunteer from Princeton in Mercer County. She is still strapped into her seat but her face and skull are crushed and she is sun-burned, heavily so at one point on her arm. Sheriff Fowler immediately dispatches the body to the morgue in Unionville. The high school students return to the Shields gas station. "Give them all they want," says George Coffey, Continental's Assistant Director for Public Relations to the staff. ". . . all the candy and all the pop and it's on us." [91, 93, 147, 149, 150, 151]

The Tail Section Crash Site
4:00 PM CT Thursday

Between the trees in Section 17 of Franklin Township in Appanoose County they are working in teams. The experts are lifting, turning, examining, and smelling the five-hundred pieces of the aircraft's skin and the thousands of surrounding fragments. They scrutinize bulges, perforations, smudges, powder burns, residue on fragments of pipes, wires, interior walls and carpeting. Under the leadership of George Van Epps, they make no assumptions. They know two facts: 1) The tail of the plane was severed in the air, and 2) The plane broke up in the air. The rest is based on careful examination, the judicious attention to details. The evidence is assembled. It's followed to logical probes. The metal skin curls outwards. If wind had been the force, it would be bent or wrinkled. A conclusion is reached, "the metal skin has been shattered by an intensive force, not wrenched apart in a storm." Weather forces are set aside. An internal explosion is considered. And ash-like particles tell the fuel experts whatever the force was—it wasn't jet fuel. Samples from fragments of curtains, seats, cushions, and carpeting are sent to FBI Headquarters in Washington DC for laboratory analysis to determine the nature of the explosive ingredient.

Standing and watching the investigation is Bob Six who is about to depart to the Continental Airlines headquarters in Denver. He turns to Don Wilson, Vice President of Flight, and the ranking Continental official at the scene. Six says, "I think this is sabotage." Don Wilson agrees.[2, 139, 149, 153]

There's another team working at the crash site. It's working separately and independently. The Hall Engineering Company of Centerville has been hired by CAB's lead investigator, George Van Epps, to survey, record, and map the location of the major pieces of Continental Flight 11's debris. The team's leader has a sterling reputation. Robert "Bob" Buss is a trained chemical engineer from Caltech with a business MA from Harvard. In World War II at the age of twenty-four he worked on the Manhattan Project assisting the team solving the complicated detonation of the plutonium (Nagasaki) bomb. Today he's leading his team with their transits and theodolites, measuring vertical and horizontal angles, running traverse lines with chains and pins, noting the shape and contour of the land, establishing distances and recording each object in their surveyor field books. [153, 154, 155]

Unionville, Missouri
4:30 PM CT Thursday

At the morgue on West Main Street, the body of Continental Flight 11's last victim, a flight hostess, has arrived. She is identified by Unionville dentist Dr. R.H. McCalment. He corresponds occlusal fillings in both lower left molars with bite-wing x-rays taken two months previously in Santa Monica, California, by a Dr. Robert C. Wallin. An appendectomy scar and her general description confirms her name, Martha Joyce Rush. A team of US Army pathologists continue her examination with Dr. Charles Judd. FBI Director Mark Felt observes the process noting Dr. Judd's focus on her arm. It's an extensive chemical burn, Judd tells him, "black and charred" caused by "flash flame" and it "appears to be by some type of chemical burn from a higher grade chemical than jet fuel." Dr. Judd has made other observations on his other Flight 11 autopsies. He found powder burns on the arms of two hostesses, shrapnel in some other victims and in one autopsy on one particular passenger he found "explosive residue." [64, 74, 82, 151]

Centerville, Iowa
5:00 PM CT Thursday

Robert Beck, the publisher and editor of the *Centerville Daily Iowegian,* is still following his assignment. He's back in Centerville from Unionville. He has talked with people of the area and writes his editorial for the next day's (Friday the 25th) newspaper. "This terrible tragedy, the loss of forty-five people, has come . . . as a severe shock to the folks of this southern Iowa and northern Missouri area."[119, 157]

Here in Centerville Beck is witnessing "the dozens," "the army of people—the world press, officials with Continental Airlines, the FBI, FAA, CAB, relatives of the deceased all looking for places to stay." He talks to Boyd O'Briant the executive secretary at Centerville's Chamber of Commerce. "Everything in town is full except for three hotel rooms." As Boyd is talking, those are quickly filled forcing Boyd to appeal to people to call him if they have extra accommodations. Seventy-five rooms are promptly offered. "This will meet our demands very nicely," says Boyd. Robert Webb the chamber president tells how Unionville with its much smaller population is working wonders finding places for people to stay . . . "but they are appealing to us for help. The two cities" he continues, "are working back and forth . . . we'll give full cooperation."

Additionally there's the world press and its technical needs. Louis Ver Baere, Centerville photographer and the *Iowegian's* press operator, vacates his studio on Centerville square's north side. Louis supervises connections for wire service operations, wire photo machines, telephones, and typewriters. Leading national journalists move in. They include United Press International's (UPI) Walter Frerck from St. Louis and Walter Brown from Des Moines. The Associated Press (AP) is represented by Bill Straeter, Robert Gallimore, and Bill Anderson, all based in Kansas City.[70, 157, 158, 159, 160]

Earlier in his assignment, Beck describes Unionville, Missouri, as the "nerve center" of the investigation. He describes Centerville as "the headquarters." And at the core of it—the fulcrum—the center of operations is the Continental Hotel on the Square's east side. It is there the CAB investigation establishes its base. The lead investigator, George Van Epps, is staying there. So is Edward Slattery, six members of the CAB, and the incoming experts.

Charles Annis, the Continental Hotel manager, gets a telephone call from New York from the editor of *Newsweek*. When was the last time "you had so much excitement around your hotel?" "Not since Jesse James was reported to have stayed at the hotel the night before he robbed the bank in Corydon." "The editor seemed to get a big kick out of that," Annis tells Beck.[158]

In the evenings in the Continental Hotel dining room all the experts meet with Van Epps. FBI agents join them from Motel 60, three blocks to the east, and so does Mark Felt who is staying with Dr. Ritter at his home on North First Street. They discuss, debate, and argue well into the night.[70, 94]

Unionville: The Morgue
9:00 PM CT Thursday

At 9:00 PM US Army pathologists release the body of the last victim to the funeral directors. Martha Joyce Rush was one of Flight 11's hostesses. She was found six-and-a-half hours earlier in the day lying in long grass on rising ground two-and-a-half miles from the main fuselage. The pathologists call for x-rays after completing their autopsy. They also endorse Dr. Charles Judd's concern about the black mark/abrasion on her arm. They tell Mark Felt the mark could be linked "to something other than weather conditions [that] caused the plane to blow apart." The information is relayed to the CAB investigative team in Centerville. The funeral directors anticipate a five hour wait for the forty-three caskets en route from Batesville, Indiana.[44, 74, 116, 152, 160]

Centerville, Iowa
10:00 PM CT Thursday

At the Continental Hotel on the square's east side, a CAB press conference is underway. Journalists and reporters are asking questions about the progress of the investigation. Charlie DePuy—still surviving on limited sleep—asks the question the other news people are eager to hear answered. Among them are Peter Reich of the *Chicago American* and John Ratterman of the *Kansas City Star*. Charlie's question: "Was any passenger heavily insured for this flight?" There is no answer. There is silence. The FBI agents are leaving. They are saying nothing.

In fact, the FBI agents have already thought of that. And one brown leather briefcase . . . the one found by Gabe Raskie one mile east of Cincinnati . . . the brown leather briefcase with three initials—TGD—on the front is beginning to play a significant role in the investigation.[128, 153]

Washington DC
11:00 PM ET Thursday

At the FBI scientific laboratories in the Justice Department building on Pennsylvania Avenue, there are more agents "saying nothing." They are analyzing the travel plans, the background of each of the thirty-seven passengers of Continental Flight 11. Two passengers—#9 and #10, a man and a woman—are emerging for special attention, especially passenger #9, Thomas Gene Doty. They were traveling together, and at Chicago O'Hare Airport prior to Flight 11's departure, both bought air flight insurance. Passenger #10, the woman, Geneva Opal Fraley bought flight insurance for $75,000. Passenger #9, Doty, also bought flight insurance for $75,000. It was his third insurance for this flight. FBI special agents in Chicago and Kansas City reveal the other two, $50,000 four days before the crash on May 18, 1962, and three days later on May 21, the day before the crash, another $225,000. The beneficiary of all $350,000 is the man's wife, Naomi Doty.

And there's more. The FBI identification division is releasing fingerprint records to help identify the victims. In 1948, aged twenty, Doty registered for the post-World War II selective service system. Diagnosed with diabetes mellitus, he's classified 4F. Fourteen years later, one month before his death on Flight 11, there's another fingerprint record. He was arrested in Kansas City, Kansas, on April 23, 1962. He was charged with "vagrancy, investigation and strong-arm robbery and carrying a concealed weapon." He was due to appear in court to answer these charges on May 25, three days after his death. For Mrs. Fraley, the elite FBI fingerprint team locate a latent (hidden) print on a bottle of perfume at her Independence, Missouri, home. She has no fingerprint record.[162]

Friday, May 25, 1962

Unionville, Missouri
2:00 AM CT Friday

The lights at the morgue on West Main Street have been shining all night. Dr. Judd, funeral directors, representatives of Continental Airlines, the FBI, and the CAB are checking and rechecking the identities of the victims. In homes across town, Unionville's Lions Club members are waiting for a telephone call from the morgue. It comes at 2:00 AM when trucks carrying forty-three Monosealer caskets arrive in Unionville from Batesville, Indiana. The Lions Club members unload the caskets. They place each identified victim into a casket and reload the truck. By 4:00 AM, twenty victims are starting to their homes via Kansas City or Chicago. The remaining twenty-three victims are still being processed.[44, 82, 148]

Centerville
9:00 AM CT Friday

Robert (Bob) Beck, the publisher and editor of the *Centerville Daily Iowegian*, arrives at the Continental Hotel on the square's east side to interview Edward Slattery, the CAB's public information officer. The subject is the breakup of the plane. Slattery tells Beck no copper wire has been found and no timing device. The force that caused Flight 11 to break up is a mystery at this stage. It wasn't metal fatigue. It wasn't a midair collision. Information is needed from the flight recorder. Was it the storms that were in the area? "Our next step," Slattery says, "is to build 'a mock-up' of the crashed 707. This calls for building a wooden frame to the exact size and proportion of the airplane. This wooden frame is then covered in chicken wire and all parts of the wreckage are placed in their correct position on the mockup. This usually shows the origin of the break-up and the procession of the break-up."[119, 163]

Beck asks where this mockup will be built. "Negotiations are underway for a hangar in Kansas City, Missouri . . . Everything here will be tagged and shipped out on lowboys." With this news, many journalists and reporters are leaving town. The reconstruction will take time. The next developments will be in Kansas City. That's before they read the *Iowegian* newspaper. The local weather report is on page two of that day's *Centerville Daily Iowegian*: "Considerable cloudiness with scattered showers and thunderstorms through Saturday. Locally heavy and most numerous thunderstorms Friday night." Slattery knows what rain will do: evidence will be obliterated. The powdery remains, the smudges, the burn spots, the distinctive odor could disappear. He leaves the Continental Hotel, walks along 13th Street to the office of Centerville Mayor Harry Dukes in City Hall on Highway 2. "Can you supply a building for five-hundred pieces of Flight 11's tail section? Can you supply it today?" Dukes and Boyd O'Briant measure the newest building at the Appanoose County Fairgrounds. It measures one-hundred-five feet long and sixty feet wide. They ask Slattery, "Will this do?"[163, 164, 165]

The same day, by afternoon ahead of the rains, the mockup of Flight 11 originally planned for a hangar in Kansas City is being erected at the Appanoose County Fairgrounds. Leo Craver at his lumberyard and his workers Red Simmons, Carl Barbaglia, and Gary Barrickman are working overtime. So is Floyd McFall of the Centerville Street Department and Appanoose County Board's men with trucks working in relays hauling the five-hundred parts of Flight 11's tail section from Section 17 of Franklin Township. Supervising the process—the handling, the lifting of each part—are head of the FAA Najeeb Halaby, Dewey Ballard, and the FAA team from Kansas City.[119, 163, 165, 166]

Unionville, Missouri
2:00 PM CT Friday

In the morgue on West Main Street relatives and friends of some of the victims are arriving. The mood is somber. There is emotion. There are tears. The visitors are met by George Coffey the Assistant Public Relations Director for Continental Airlines and Putnam County Sheriff David Fowler. Breaking from his almost insurmountable paperwork of three death certificates for each of the forty-five victims—double that for insurance claims, is Dr. Charles Judd. He meets every visitor.[168]

Among the first arrivals are the father and relatives of a boy from Illinois. They confirm the boy's identity in ten minutes. Jim Updyke of Updyke Motors of Kirksville identifies the three Chrysler Corporation Executives. The three, says Jim Updyke, were on their way to a meeting in Kansas City, a meeting he and his wife were planning to attend. He tells the story of one of the three, Fred Herman, an immigrant from Czechoslovakia. Herman volunteered for service in the US Army following Pearl Harbor. He survived the Bataan Death March, spent four years in a Japanese prisoner of war camp, then died on a Missouri alfalfa hillside. From London, England, Mr. R.E.G. Windsor, the chairman and managing director of R.H. Windsor Ltd, Chessington, Surrey, identifies Philip Ireland Hoare. The man, he says, born in Cardiff, Wales, was his assistant chief engineer, his most trusted employee. From New York City, where he's the manager of an export firm, Yataro Shoji arrives with flowers to place near the body of Takehiko Nakano. Takehiko, he says, was an expert service manager for electronic microscopes and the best of good friends. In the Japanese tradition, he will travel with the body back to his home in Tokyo. In response to a request from the Nakano family for the place of death of Takehiko, Charlie DePuy provides a map of Centerville. On it Charlie marks St. Joseph Mercy Hospital.[124, 169]

Centerville, Iowa
6:00 PM CT Friday

Two men are facing each other across a dinner table at the Green Circle restaurant on Centerville's south side. One is Don Wilson, Continental Airlines Vice-President of Flight. The other, Edward Slattery, the Information Officer for the Civil Aeronautics Board. Their discussion is heated. Their voices are raised. Wilson wants the CAB to announce that what happened on board Flight 11 was an explosion. Continental Airlines experts—thirty of them—have examined the debris and have no doubt some sort of explosion brought down the aircraft. Edward Slattery is holding back. He doesn't want to "shoot from the hip." He wants to wait for the analysis of the flight recorder. Bad weather cannot be ruled out. Wilson knows Slattery holds the power. The CAB is an arm of the US Government. It controls the schedules, the fares, the routes traveled by all US airlines, and that includes Continental's. And it's for the CAB report—its authority—citing the cause of the crash, that the world awaits. The discussion according to others in the restaurant is becoming louder.[149]

Centerville, Iowa
7:00 PM CT Friday

John Ratterman is a reporter for the *Kansas City Star*. He's based in Centerville. For days he's been working his sources, digging, checking, listening, and writing. He's just had information from Denver. At the Continental Airlines headquarters executives are announcing they "are of the opinion that some 'man-made condition' caused the airplane to disintegrate and plummet to earth . . . ." Ratterman submits his article to the *Star*, its title, "Jet Probe Aim on Blast." He subtitles it "See Man-Made Cause." The *Kansas City Star* is the first newspaper in the US to move the cause of Flight 11's crash from speculation to theory to the suggestion that it was a bomb that brought the plane down. The *Kansas City Star* copyrights Ratterman's story. A day later the *Chicago American* upstages the *Kansas City Star*. Their writer, Peter Reich, who "never wrote a sentence he didn't believe to be true," headlines his article "Murder—Suicide."

After submitting his article, Ratterman is driving south to Unionville, Missouri, on Highway 5(60). At the morgue on West Main Street the last three bodies are about to leave. Flowers sent by relatives are wilting at the window. The streets, roped off since Wednesday, are open again to traffic. Ratterman drives six miles north to the fuselage remains of Flight 11 at the Shuey Field. National Guardsmen from Kirksville's Howitzer 2 Battalion are standing guard. Continental Airlines employees have removed most of the personal effects. But some remain . . . a crushed and battered uniform cap with the Continental insignia, a flight manual, a graph for emergency procedures for extreme turbulence, magazines in stiff blue binders, a notepad with scores from a card game, a set of twisted golf clubs, a briefcase, a prayer book, and a toothbrush.[170]

Centerville Town Square
9:00 PM CT Friday

Edward Slattery is arriving back at the Continental Hotel after his dinner at the Green Circle Restaurant. He joins George Van Epps, the head of the CAB Investigation, members of the CAB team, and the FBI's Mark Felt at a meeting underway in a private room. More FBI agents are arriving. One carries into the room a crescent-shaped piece of metal in a plastic bag; another brings a piece of crumpled, torn, yellow tubing two feet in length, an inch in diameter. Both items have been found near Centerville. Under discussion at the meeting is the progress of the investigation. John F. Pahl the Chief Investigative Engineer, Bureau of Safety of the Civil Aeronautics Board, reports conclusively: damage to the aircraft has been caused by a high order explosive in the tail section of the aircraft. He reveals a small piece of paper found by his investigators at the crash scene. It is waxy. It is browny-beige in color. On it are two letters, "D" and part of a letter "A." For these professional investigators the waxy paper, the torn yellow tubing, are significant. They resemble the wrapping around dynamite sticks and a fuse. The tone of this conference is changing. For Mark Felt his role and that of his agents is shifting. It is moving from identifying the bodies to investigating a crime: one of mass murder.[156, 171]

The Continental Hotel
10:30 PM CT Friday

Edward Slattery is alone with George Van Epps. They are worrying. The two decide to issue a statement on the investigation before there's a lot of speculation and mis-information. This statement will include the word "explosion" and include it even though the flight recorder information has not yet been released to them.

Alone in his room Slattery writes the statement on Hotel Continental stationery.

"CAB air safety investigators have determined an explosive force of unknown origin occurred within the aft portion of the fuselage and caused the aircraft to break up in flight."

He submits it to the CAB Headquarters in Washington, DC.

Sleep for Slattery this night is evasive. He hears the Appanoose County Courthouse clock strike the hours. When sleep comes, it's uneasy.[171]

Saturday, May 26, 1962

Centerville, Iowa
5:45 AM CT Saturday

From his room at the Continental Hotel Edward Slattery phones the CAB headquarters office on Dupont Circle in Washington, DC. He strongly recommends the release of the statement he's submitted.[149]

The Continental Hotel
10:15 AM CT Saturday

Slattery is waiting for a response from the CAB Head Office. It comes at 10:15 Central Time—four and a half hours after submitting his statement. The speaker is CAB Chairman Alan S. Boyd. After a meeting of the five CAB members, Slattery's statement is approved without a single word changed. In addition Boyd tells Slattery the flight recorder report has been released. It reveals Continental Flight 11 was five minutes beyond any weather turbulence.

Slattery again lifts the telephone. He calls *Associated Press, United Press International*, the *Centerville Daily Iowegian* and the *Unionville Republican* in that precise order. He reads them what now is his official statement. Then he waits for all the new excitement. It isn't long in coming. The news is flashing across screens across the country. The press, radio, and TV reporters are making their way, converging back to Centerville. Slattery anticipates an afternoon conference.[128, 149]

Kansas City, Kansas
9:00 AM CT Saturday

FBI Investigative work in Kansas City begins. The focus is on passenger #9: Thomas Gene Doty. FBI Special Agent Otto T. Handwerk is visiting the Kansas City, Kansas, Police Department's Record Bureau. He is advised ". . . Thomas Gene Doty, a white, male, born April 17, 1928 at San Antonio, Texas, was arrested April 23, 1962 and charged with vagrancy, investigation and strong-arm robbery and carrying a concealed weapon." A search of their records discloses no prior arrest of Mr. Doty. The details of the arrest are redacted.[172]

Kansas City, Kansas
9:30 AM CT Saturday

The Wyandotte County Attorney, Kansas City, Kansas, is advising Special Agent Handwerk. Because of the death of Thomas Doty on Flight 11, his case was dismissed May 25, 1962, in city court. His prosecution file against Mr. Doty is available. The attorney representing Mr. Doty has his office at 388 New Brotherhood Building in Kansas City, Kansas, says the County Attorney.[173]

Kansas City, Kansas
10:00 AM CT Saturday

Special Agent Handwerk is at room 388 of the New Brotherhood Building. He is meeting with the attorney [name redacted] representing Thomas Doty. On the night of his arrest Doty told his attorney he had been drinking at the Keg Bar and the Old Heidelberg Inn, both in Kansas City, Missouri. While enroute home he became ill, parked his car on Rainbow Boulevard, just south of 39th Street, and walked around the block where he vomited. He was carrying a .22 caliber nine-shot revolver, taking it from his car which could not be locked. Just prior to being captured he had picked up a woman's purse which was lying on the ground. He claimed he had not robbed the woman victim and had not entered her car.

The attorney tells Special Agent Handwerk he could have won an acquittal for Doty.[174]

Centerville
10:00 AM CT Saturday

At one end of the one-hundred-fifty-foot fairgrounds building on the northwest edge of Centerville, less than a mile from the Continental Hotel, Robert Beck, the *Daily Iowegian's* editor, is watching the reconstruction of Flight 11's tail section. It's the upper part of the tail from one foot above the craft's floor. In charge of the mock-up is John S. Leak the CAB's Chief Structural Engineer. Alongside him are representatives of the Boeing Aircraft Company and a four-foot stack of 707 construction manuals they brought with them from Seattle. Timber, much of it cut into 2x4 foot sections, rolls of chicken wire, screws, nails, and twine are being constantly delivered by Gary Barrickman from Leo Craver's lumber yard on Highway 2. Carpenters Red Simmons and Carl Barbaglia recreate the empennage, the twenty-feet from the rear cabin door to the tail end. They are following instructions from John Leak and the Boeing representatives. The work, observes Beck, is proceeding "feverishly."[24, 121, 149, 153]

At the other end of the building the head of the FAA, Najeeb Halaby, and his team from Kansas City under Dewey Ballard are arranging broken suitcases, clothes, and the shoes of the victims.[149]

Kansas City, Missouri
10:40 AM CT Saturday

At 10:40 AM a telephone is ringing in the Kansas City FBI office of Special Agent Royal Perkins. The speaker is a man. He says he has pertinent information into the crash of Continental Flight 11 and wishes to meet with an FBI Agent. Forty minutes later at 11:20 AM, the speaker arrives at Perkins' office. The man—[name redacted] gives his place of residence as Silver Springs, Maryland. He arrived in Kansas City from Baltimore at 9:05 PM the night before, Friday May 25. He came to join his wife who'd flown earlier on Friday reaching Kansas City in the late morning. They are staying at the home of Naomi Doty whose husband Tom died aboard Flight 11. This Saturday morning at 4:30 AM he was awakened by [name redacted] who was upset at a conversation with Naomi Doty the day before.

Between 6:00 AM and 7:00 AM this morning, the man had a lengthy discussion with Naomi Doty about that conversation the previous day. It is this conversation that has brought him to FBI Agent Perkins. Mrs. Doty, he reports, communicated nine specific concerns, incidents, events, and words spoken to her by her husband Tom Doty. Seven of the nine are heavily redacted. Two less so. One of these is her description of seeing a briefcase in their car and inside it "foreign material." Another of Mrs. Doty's concerns was that no member of the family had viewed her husband's body. The man speaking to Agent Perkins said he performed this function with her approval at the funeral home prior to his phone call to Agent Perkins. He recognized Tom Doty by "the physical size, color of his hair, bushy eyebrows, etc." He observed nothing which would lead him to believe the body is not that of Doty.

In the morning conversation with Naomi Doty the man suggested the information she had should be turned over to the FBI, and she agreed. She wishes to do this as soon as possible. She will contact her attorney and Agent Perkins for an interview tomorrow. She also will allow a search to be made of her home and of the family cars.[175]

Centerville
2:30 PM CT Saturday

Charlie DePuy is back at The Continental Hotel. It's been over three hours since Edward Slattery's telephoned announcement to *AP, UPI*, the *Iowegian,* and the *Unionville Republican* with his electrifying inclusion of the word "explosion" as the cause of the Flight 11 crash. In three hours, the press is back in force, and Slattery is holding a press conference. He sits in the hotel lobby alongside the fireplace. Newsmen are taking notes. Photographers are recording the scene.[199]

"From the very first" says Slattery, "we were highly suspicious of an explosive force." But metal fatigue, a mid-air collision, weather turbulence had to be eliminated. There have been heated discussions. Continental Airlines' thirty people, many of them metal experts, knew their first day on the job it was an explosion. The FBI believed there was "something more" as they did their routine body identifications. The CAB specialists found the turbulence theory unacceptable, but they wanted to learn from the flight recorder. This has now been done. The recorder shows Flight 11 was a full five minutes beyond any bad weather. It was flying at its designated thirty-nine-thousand feet. The explosion occurred in the aft section. The evidence the explosion left in the break near the tail section is what aroused suspicions. Metal bends if air forces cause disintegration. But the metal on Flight 11 is "torn" as if "blown to pieces." The metal edges indicate an intense force not a bending force. And there are smudges bearing a distinct odor. There are small metal particles in the seat cushions and curtains and in the skin of some victims. There is residue in pipes, interior walls, carpeting, and ash in the conditioning system. A voice from the press representatives present says, "Why not call it a bomb?" The ever-careful Slattery answers, "That's what you say, but I only stay with my statement." He adds that the FBI has re-entered the case because of the possibility of criminal aspects. "This is a terrible thing, you know."[153, 163]

Centerville: The Fairgrounds Building
3:30 PM CT Saturday

By late afternoon progress on the reconstruction of Continental Flight 11's tail section is rapid. Del Borer, photographer for the next day's *Des Moines Sunday Register,* captures the scene. Experts from the CAB, the FBI, and explosives experts are standing, crouching, examining, and discussing some of the five-hundred large pieces of the aircraft's tail section. In the center, Centerville's Gary Barrickman is waiting for instructions to place the pieces onto the chicken-wire mockup.

The FBI's Mark Felt is noting the main portion of the fuselage is in large pieces. But behind the separation point, the pieces are progressively smaller. The last six feet of the aft are where there were some seats, the galley, the coat rack, a lavatory. And some of this is missing—the area of the right toilet. To Felt, finding the big pieces has been easy. Finding the small pieces will be difficult. The Boeing representatives working with their experts describe to Felt what needs to be found. He later writes "We [FBI Agents and Felt] had to go out and find them over a stretch of Iowa countryside ten miles wide and forty miles long. This turned out to be one of the most massive crime scene searches ever conducted by the FBI." And Felt knows he cannot do it alone.[107]

Merriam, Kansas
4:45 PM CT Saturday

FBI Special Agent Weeter S. Pond with one, possibly two additional agents [names redacted] are arriving to search the home of Naomi Doty on West 71st Terrace. This is the home she shared with her husband, Tom Doty. At the outset she is informed of her constitutional right to refuse such a search without a warrant. She replies that she's willing the search be made. She is given a "Consent to Search" form. She reads the document and signs her name at 4:54 PM. She requests to leave the home as the search occurs. A relative [name redacted] remains to represent the family.

The search is completed at 8:13 PM. The agents have made notes of routine papers, correspondence, social security cards, and pamphlets. In the closet of the master bedroom they examined guns. They found nothing in the basement "which might prove pertinent to this investigation." But in the garage they found boxes on a shelf that contain items that could well make that connection. They include synchrons, wires, some with colored clips attached, a toggle switch, a transformer, aluminum tubes, light sockets, rubber caps, a reamer, two stove bolts, light globes, nuts, washers, and a small spring. A receipt for all items is given to Mrs. Doty. The agents will return the next day, the morning of May 27, 1962, to search the automobiles away from the residence.[178]

Unionville, Missouri
9:00 PM CT Saturday

Thirty-seven members of Company A US 5th Engineers under Lieutenant Wearing are arriving in Unionville. They have traveled two-hundred-forty-seven miles north from Ft. Leonard Wood, the Army Training Base southwest of Rolla in the Missouri Ozarks. They are being quartered in the Unionville High School gymnasium. They are sleeping on cots and within seven hours will relieve the National Guard Unit of Kirksville which will return home. Company A 5th Engineers will then stand guard over the fuselage of Flight 11 and over all the restricted area. No one without a proper permit will be permitted inside.[179]

Sunday, May 27, 1962

Across America
8:00 AM CT Sunday

By Sunday morning across the country Edward Slattery's selection of the word "EXPLOSION" as an explanation for Flight 11's crash is being supplanted. In every major newspaper from Honolulu to Los Angeles, Oakland, and Sacramento on the West Coast, to Miami and Boston on the East, to the *St. Louis Post-Dispatch*, and the *Sunday Des Moines Register* in the Midwest, the new word is "BOMB." But it's Peter Reich's "MURDER—SUICIDE" *Chicago American* headline that is the talk of the country.[180, 181, 182, 183, 184, 185, 186, 187, 188]

Merriam, Kansas
9:00 AM CT Sunday

Two special agents, Royal Perkins and one other [name redacted], are returning to the Doty home on West 71st Terrace. With Naomi Doty's written permission, they remove the two cars owned by the Dotys. They begin the search the vehicles in the parking lot of the Western Electric Company in Merriam.

They start with a 1951 six-cylinder, two door white Pontiac sedan. On the back seat the agents find items that they describe as "maybe" significant. They are a *Saturday Evening Post* magazine, two bank checks, one "non-sufficient fund" check, statements from two sets of attorneys; a wallet containing a diabetic card indicating Thomas Doty, the holder. needed "NPH" insulin, two boxes of stationery with the heading "Gracious Homes, Inc.," and notice of a couple of completed fire checks of 3652 Campbell, one of Tom Doty's other houses. No further evidence is found of importance in this investigation. The second car is an all-white two-door 1962 Ford Fairlane 500. It has red upholstery, white sidewall tires, bucket seats, a radio, and a heater. The agents find a box in the glove compartment that at one time contained a prescription for Tom Doty with the direction "inject 1 cc for nausea and vomiting and repeat every four hours." In the trunk there is unopened mail addressed to individuals in Kansas City, Missouri. [All names redacted.] Nothing else was found of any pertinence.[189]

The Crash Site
9:30 AM CT Sunday

At the Shuey Field there is new tension between the Missouri and Iowa authorities. Two days previously because of pending stormy weather, the CAB ordered plane parts to be taken north to be reassembled at the Appanoose County Fair Building in Centerville. The distinction between "plane parts" and "tail section parts" was not defined. Trucks from the Centerville Street Department and the Appanoose County Board had already moved north the five-hundred pieces of the tail section—all of them lying in Iowa. When the trucks return to the Shuey field and, without permission to move the fuselage, Sheriff David Fowler intervenes. Since the CAB was the sole authority over Continental Flight 11, he contacts George Van Epps at Centerville's Continental Hotel. Van Epps emphatically denies giving such permission to anyone. The trucks return empty to Centerville.[5]

Over Appanoose County
10:00 AM CT Sunday

FBI head Mark Felt is sitting on a chair with no arms, suspended from a helicopter with no doors, flying over Appanoose County. He's looking straight down. He's searching for missing pieces of the aft of Flight 11—those critical last six feet, Flight 11's rear right lavatory. Each time he sees possible wreckage he radios the pilot. The pilot flies lower and directs ground crews to retrieve the object. On several occasions this "superb pilot," as Felt describes him, flies so low he brings the helicopter underneath the foliage of one of the large oak trees that grow in this sylvan land. The search follows the path of Flight 11's debris. It stretches from the Shuey Field to Lake Wapello in Davis County, Iowa, a distance forty-miles long and ten miles wide.

In preparation, Felt has plotted the area into a grid pattern to keep track of what has been examined and what remains to be done. He uses two helicopters with flight crews. They are in radio contact with ground search crews of two enlisted men driving four-wheel-drive jeeps. As each piece of wreckage is collected it is replaced by a numbered lath. It's a long process. Each discovered piece is taken to the county fair building in Centerville and placed on the mock-up. Edward Slattery is watching. All the recovered pieces are valuable, "Especially one piece," he says, ". . . it fitted right into the pattern of the explosion . . . like a hand in a glove."[107, 190]

Odessa, Texas
11:00 AM CT Sunday

A team of CAB Investigators is arriving in Odessa, checking into a motel and making straight for the Hubbard-Kelly Funeral Home on 6th and Alleghany Avenue. The team's focus: to examine and x-ray the body of Joyce Rush, the twenty-three-year-old stewardess aboard Continental Flight 11, before her funeral the next day. When the fatal explosion—now explicitly called a bomb—occurred, it was Tuesday, May 22, at 9:17 and 7 seconds PM. It caused the tail section to separate and fall from the main fuselage. Eight victims fell with it. Seven of the eight were found scattered across Putnam County land the next morning. The eighth was Joyce Rush. She was found at 3:25 PM the afternoon of Thursday May 24. She's found by peace officers, Unionville, and other Missouri high school seniors, juniors, and some sophomore students, walking side by side, some holding hands. She was lying in knee-high grass on what is known as Kozad Park. She was immediately flown for examination and autopsy to the morgue in Unionville.

When Joyce Rush was released from Unionville, US Pathologists requested her body be x-rayed, and Dr. Charles Judd asked for closer scrutiny on the extensive black mark on her arm. The day-long examination in Odessa this Sunday is fruitful. Joyce's body holds metal fragments. And from her arm, the black mark that concerned Dr. Judd, a tiny piece of paper is extracted. It is waxy. It is browny-beige in color. And it matches the same piece of waxy paper found by the FBI investigators back at the crash site in Missouri.[191, 192]

Eastern Appanoose County
Noon CT Sunday

Mount Ararat Baptist Church with its tall bell tower and stucco exterior has been serving the people of southeastern Appanoose County since 1868. Today is no exception. The church, the sur-rounding area it serves, and this land farmed by its congregation all lie directly below the flight path of Continental Flight 11. It is noon. Services are over. Members of the church are delaying their depar-ture. They are friends and good neighbors and the tragedy of Flight 11 is their shared experience. They talk of FBI agents they've seen in the area, the sounds of helicopters overhead, items fallen from the doomed aircraft found on their land. East of Udell, on Frank Stajcar's farm, they found a woman's coat. On Laurel Bryant's, blankets bearing the Continental Airlines crest. In a field north of Udell a suit-coat torn in half, the sleeves turned inside out, a name—T. Doty on one, and inside a pocket, seven keys on a ring. People are nervous, apprehensive about what's next. Could they find a body? Or bits of bodies? Herb Guernsey lights a cigarette.[77, 173]

People are beginning to move, to drive, to return to their homes—east towards Moulton, south to Sedan, north to Unionville, Iowa, nine miles away, or eight miles north to Udell. This will be the direction of the Cridlebaugh family, to their farm north of Udell. But today it's Sunday. They are taking a detour for their summer Sunday special. There are five of them: Lois, Raymond (he's known as "Johnny") and their three children – Kay (thirteen), Gary (eleven) and Kathy (eight). They are on their way for a sandwich luncheon at Geraldine's their favorite Drive-In Restaurant six miles west in Centerville.[77, 174]

Kansas City, Missouri
1:20 pm CT Sunday

At the Kansas City FBI Office in the Federal Courthouse on Grand Avenue, FBI Special Agents Royal Perkins and James Glonek are anticipating the arrival of Naomi Doty. Her information, outlined by [name redacted] the previous day could break wide open this investigation into the cause of Flight 11's crash. At 1:20 PM they learn Mrs. Doty has just concluded a conference with her attorney [name redacted]. She will appear at the FBI office in the next thirty minutes.[197]

Centerville
1:30 PM CT Sunday

In Centerville, thirteen-year-old Nancy Niday is walking with her family to the Appanoose County Fairground building. The family's Sunday meal is complete. Nancy's father and uncle are returning to work on the mock-up of Flight 11's tail section. "Does anyone want to look inside?" they ask. Everyone says "no." Nancy says "yes." She enters at the far end of the building. Everywhere she sees broken suitcases, clothes emerging, some spread out on top. And on a long shelf in sharp contrast is an organized line of shoes. Each shoe is with its partner. Each pair is parallel to the next with military precision. Nancy is disturbed. The shoes look ready to be stepped into, to be occupied, to be walked in, to be used by their owners . . . owners who are now dead.[198]

Udell, Iowa
1:40 PM CT Sunday

It's when the Cridlebaugh family members arrive home from Centerville they note something is different. Eleven-year-old Gary with his love of cars sees his Grandfather's green 1950 Plymouth parked in their driveway. And there is Grandfather—Pervis Cridlebaugh—walking towards them with a shotgun. Raymond looks at his eighty-one-year-old father and wonders if he's suddenly "lost it." "Dad! What the hell are you doing?" His father replies, "There's a murderer loose here. He's shot and killed five up at Martinsburg in Keokuk County. He's run out of gas and left his car on your Uncle Glenn's property. He's taken off on foot. He could be anywhere."[77]

Kansas City
1:50 PM CT Sunday

Mrs. Naomi Doty is arriving at the FBI Office. She is advised she is not required to make any statement which could be incriminating and used against her in a court of law. She is also advised of her right to consult a lawyer. Mrs. Doty identifies herself as the wife of Thomas Gene Doty, who died in the crash of Continental Flight 11 on the evening of May 22, 1962. She then states her motivation for speaking to the FBI. She says she's read newspaper accounts suggesting the plane may have been sabotaged. She feels it her duty, her responsibility, for the lives of so many people who died to furnish all the information at her disposal.

She begins with two pivotal memories. The first is a list of books [titles redacted] she has seen her husband reading since "the fall of 1961," some eight months before the crash. She names three libraries where her husband could have obtained them: Linda Hall, Johnson County, and Westport. The second memory is "one or one-and-one-half months ago." Then she saw two items [redacted] inside a brown leather briefcase inside the open trunk of their 1951 Pontiac parked in their driveway. It was the same briefcase she saw her husband take with him when he flew to Chicago from Kansas City on the morning of May 21, 1962, the day before the crash. Mrs. Doty describes the briefcase, "medium brown in color, approximately fourteen inches or fifteen inches in length and approximately twelve inches high . . . [with] a snap type latch on top as opposed to a zipper." Mrs. Doty proceeds with Tom Doty's medical history. He was diabetic since he was sixteen or seventeen years of age. She gives details of his immediate family, his employment (six places including his new enterprise of Gracious Homes), his education, the rental properties they own, their sources of income, their bank accounts (there are five), stocks they own, and all liabilities including credit cards. She also talks about her husband's moods and his drinking habits.

Thirty-five-year-old Naomi Doty, just five days since the death of her husband, at the end of what she describes as a good marriage, the mother of their five-year-old daughter and seven months pregnant with their second child, provides knowledge that fills twenty-one pages of the FBI official report. And Naomi Doty has done much more. Her information has provided a road map for FBI agents for the next three weeks. Mark Felt's agents now prepare to check, to follow, to investigate, to examine and deduce, if Thomas Gene Doty is the suicide bomber that brought down Continental Flight 11.[197]

Udell, Iowa
2:00 PM CT Sunday

Accused murderer Gayno Smith's abandoned car is standing one to one-and-a-half miles north of Udell on the land of Gene Cridle-baugh. It's a dark blue/black 1950 Lincoln. The license plate reads 54 (Keokuk County) 3393. The Sheriff and Police of Keokuk County are alongside the car. So is Appanoose County Sheriff, Paul Thomas, and Deputy Harry Robertson. The Keokuk County Sheriff, John Wallerich, knows who he's looking for—twenty-four-year-old Gayno Smith. The suspect is 5'8" in height, weighs 155-165 pounds, has brown hair with a "butch" haircut, and wears thick glasses. Late Saturday night or early Sunday morning he shot and killed five members of the McBeth family—his uncle, aunt, and three cousins. One cousin, a fifteen-year-old, escaped and ran to a nearby farm for help. Gayno Smith drove away. He drove sixty miles south and west, taking back roads to avoid discovery, through Albia, through Moravia, through Hiattsville where the three Dooley children (Alan, Ray, and Susan) wave to him. At the deserted car Sheriff Wallerich finds a blood-stained flashlight under the driver's seat. Footprints are leading west into the timberland. Gayno Smith, says Sheriff Waller-ich, will be carrying a box of ammunition and a gun—the gun he used to kill five members of the McBeth family. It's an "over-under gun" —a combination 410 shotgun and 22 rifle. "Gayno" as the Sheriff calls him, is an ex-marine. He's known to be an "amazing shot."[201, 203, 206, 224, 233]

Across Udell, neighbor is calling neighbor. Police are going door to door. Sixty-two-year-old Willie Gorden, home from Unionville's Brethren Church, is working in his yard. Willie is a World War I hero. He's a recipient of the Silver Star for repeatedly saving gassed soldiers at the deadly Meuse-Argonne Offensive despite being gassed himself. He's approached by a police officer who asks him about the killer. "After that" Willie tells reporter Arden Wilson, "I was plenty scared." So too is Glenn Cridlebaugh who survived World War II's Battle of the Bulge and sees Gayno Smith's car on his land.[77, 204, 205, 206, 224]

Centerville, Iowa
2:15 PM CT Sunday

For some time a red light has been beaming from the rooftop of the Appanoose County Courthouse. It's the signal for members of Sheriff Thomas's posse to join the sheriff. Everyone is exhausted. For more than five days they've been helping at the Flight 11 disaster field. They've been searching for debris across forty miles from the Shuey field to Lake Wapello. They've been on twenty-four-hour guard protecting the mock-up of Continental Flight 11's tail section at the Appanoose County Fair building. Wayne Sheston who's been checking alleyways and Ronnie Robertson the police recruit make the drive to Udell. Being a member of the posse is voluntary work and it's unpaid. Ben Mease, one of Centerville's bankers says, "This is more than we bargained for when we joined the posse."[195, 196]

Udell, Iowa
2:30 PM CT Sunday

Sheriffs and their posses from surrounding counties (Davis, Wayne, Monroe, Wapello, Mahaska, Jefferson), all heavily armed, are moving into the deep timberland. Overhead they are aided by four army helicopters directed from Flight 11's investigation by FBI's Mark Felt. Helping in the air too is Bill Minor with his private plane equipped with a radio. Those on the ground area begin searching every building. Following the direction of the footprints, the Tubaugh Brothers Farm, two-and-a-half miles west, is searched. All windows and exits are sealed and nailed shut. A mile further west at the Moffitt empty farmhouse, Iowa Highway Patrolman Don Ruppert, of Burlington, feels confident Gayno is inside. Bloodhounds arrive to give confirmation but they "prove ineffective."[206, 207]

State highway patrol officers are receiving bulletins and directives from Sgt. Mike "Jack" Beaman at the Des Moines office. Road blocks are to be placed on all roads. Cars are to be posted at all intersections. Gas stations are to be alerted with descriptions of Gayno Smith. The possibility of hostages being taken becomes the focus of Officer Tom Simpson of Burlington. Drivers are advised, "Don't pick up a hitch hiker," and "Don't take any risks."[208]

Centerville
3:00 PM CT Sunday

In the main part of the fairgrounds building the assembling of the tail section mock-up is advancing. More pieces are arriving. Some fragments are white and porcelain brought from Felt's FBI helicopter search on the forty-mile debris path from the Shuey Field to Lake Wapello. Boeing engineers are identifying each piece. They are hanging or pasting each piece into its correct location. What is emerging is a gap, a space in the right rear fuselage. CAB engineers W. Peterson and D.C. Valle say, "It's looking more and more like a hole." The CAB's Senior Structural Specialist, John S. Leak, is measuring the diameter: it's two-hundred-twenty inches. It's in the location of the right rear lavatory used by men and women. George Van Epps and Edward Slattery, confident with their findings, announce a press conference for tomorrow, May 28. It will be at the fairgrounds building. It will begin at 9:00 AM.[163, 171, 200]

Udell and Unionville, Iowa
5:30 PM CT Sunday

Nightfall is approaching. Unionville, Iowa, is made relatively safe when the American Legion Hall is declared search headquarters and becomes the base for hundreds of law enforcement officers. As an all-night event is becoming clear, Centerville's Salvation Army volunteers arrive with sandwiches and coffee.[206, 207]

But for the people living in the area around Unionville and Udell, this will be a memorable night. They are locking their doors and latching their windows. They are removing all keys from their vehicles. They are keeping on all yard lights and know not to admit any stranger into their houses. Some are leaving the area, but for any farmer this is only an overnight solution. Some are sending their children to stay with distant relatives. Joe Wilson who farms three miles north of Unionville on the Unionville-Blakesburg Road takes his wife and four children—Becky (sixteen), Mary Jo (thirteen), Dan (ten), and Beth (six)—into Unionville to stay with relatives John and Helen Harrington. Joe, a fighter pilot in the Pacific in World War II, returns to his farm with his 12-gauge shotgun at hand throughout the night. Many families drive with their children to sleep in their cars near the American Legion Hall in Unionville or close to Gayno Smith's car—both places they know are well protected by officers. The three Dooley children who'd waved to Gayno Smith as he drove—and slowed down—by their home in Hiattsville, recognize him on television news reports that night. The Dooley family members cover every window with blankets, eliminating even a crack of light. Their father sleeps with a loaded gun under his bed and so does fourteen-year-old Alan.[201, 209]

Darkness arrives. "The people are really frightened," says Appanoose County Sheriff Paul Thomas, "and you can't blame them."[206]

Street lights, normally turned off at midnight, burn through the night.[206, 207]

Monday, May 28, 1962

Centerville, Iowa
9:00 AM CT Monday

The Civil Aeronautics Board Press Conference scheduled for 9:00 AM at the fairgrounds building begins promptly on time. Three top CAB Investigators, George Van Epps, Chief of the Bureau of Safety; John Leak, Senior Structural Specialist; and Edward Slattery, Public Relations Officer, prepare to reveal what caused the Boeing 707, Continental Flight 11 to crash killing all forty-five people on board. Press offices in Paris, London, and New York are poised ready to hear this news from Centerville, Iowa. At the Appanoose County Fairgrounds building so are fifteen to thirty newsmen, cameramen, television, and radio representatives . . . among them Charlie DePuy and Bob Beck of the *Centerville Daily Iowegian*; Mervin Nelson from the *Des Moines Register*; *United Press International's* George Brown; and from the Kansas City office of *Associated Press*, Bob Gallimore.[161, 199]

Van Epps, Leak, and Slattery, together with CAB engineers W. Peterson and D.C. Valle, guide the news reporters to the right rear side of the mock-up. The cause of Flight 11's crash is quickly revealed and is obvious. There is a hole. A two-hundred-twenty-inch hole twelve feet from the cone (the tip end) of the tail at the right rear lavatory. A hole that tore the metal outwards with such force the metal was propelled straight out over rivet heads. The fin and the tail section were then violently separated from the fuselage. John Leak points to the jagged edges of the metal. He explains,

"When metal breaks outward it is indicated on the metal by a TEAR. The molecular separation is different. The metal when caused by a powerful force such as a storm BENDS." The force here, he continues, was a high velocity explosion. Accompanying it was a distinctive odor. Soon FBI analysts at the laboratory in Washington DC will name the chemical composition. It was a bomb, and it was lit by a fuse. No copper wire, no timing devices have been found. John Leak speculates "the bomber went to the right rear lavatory, placed the explosive device in the towel bin, lit the fuse, and returned to his seat." Leak and Slattery point to darkened areas, smudges and residue on metal exposed to the blast. "It resembles black dottle" says Slattery, "or thick stuff in a pipe bowl smeared on a flat surface."

Questions are directed to George Van Epps, the CAB chief investigator. "Is there any significance in the briefcase found on the Gabe Raskie farm near Cincinnati after the crash?" Van Epps nods. "It might be significant." "Could it have been used to carry an explosive aboard the plane?" He answers, "It would have been possible . . . The briefcase is about to be sent to the FBI Laboratory to expose and possibly confirm explosive residue inside it."

Some distance away inside the same fairground building the reporters are shown a second mock-up. It's a reconstruction of the inside of the tail section created with whatever material that has been recovered. There the reporters view the galley, the cupboard behind it, the coat rack, and two tri-cornered lavatories. The white porcelain appliances of one are shattered almost to powder.[199, 200, 210, 211, 212, 213, 224]

The Udell/Unionville, Iowa area
10:00 AM CT Monday

At the Lloyd Moffitt Farm three-and-a-half miles west of Unionville, Iowa, Appanoose County Sheriff Paul Thomas, Deputy Sheriff Harry Robertson, and the posse have been awake all night. They are circling the building, out of sight, waiting for Gayno to emerge. There is no Gayno. One mile east of the Moffitt Farm, one mile closer to Unionville at the Tubaugh Brothers Farm that was searched, sealed, and nailed shut the night before, a rear door is open. Surrounding it is a scattering of nails. This house, repeatedly enlarged and altered with changing attic sections, is where Gayno has spent the night. Captain Louis Dean of the Iowa Highway Patrol withdraws all but a skeleton crew from the Moffitt Farm.[214]

Farmers going out early to their chores are carrying shotguns. They are hesitant to get into their isolated fields with a killer at large. For the law enforcement officers the search is methodical and wary. They are all heavily armed. Seven exhausted members of the Appanoose sheriff's posse—Lionel Spring, Ted Clark, Frank Stajcar, Wayne Sheston, Bob Bozwell, Mick Kruzich, and Richard Tracy—wait for instructions. Four army helicopters are again released by Mark Felt of the FBI from their Continental Flight 11 investigative duties. Each helicopter is equipped with a walkie talkie to contact ground control. Local pilot Bill Minor in his private plane with radio communication again volunteers extra assistance.[214, 215, 224, 225, 226, 228]

Kansas City, Kansas
11:00 AM CT Monday

FBI Special Agents Otto Handwerk and Joseph Kelly are interviewing the Kansas City, Kansas, police officers and patrolmen involved in the April 23, 1962, arrest of Thomas Doty. [All names redacted.] They learn a radio call was received by police officers at 11:30 PM that night. It came from two men who had apprehended a third man at 39th and Rainbow Streets. A woman claimed the man—Doty—had forced his way into her car, struck her, and taken her purse. Doty denied her accusations. When the police arrived Doty told them he had been drinking. He was not drunk and all the police officers agreed he was not drunk. Doty continued, saying he stopped his car on Rainbow just south of 39th Street because he felt ill. He was walking the block, saw a woman's purse, picked it up, and was then held by two men waiting for the police. Although Doty was not drunk and perfectly lucid, the officers noted Doty was responding to questions "slowly." He would "stare off into space," did not always "appear to be listening." One uses the word "dopey," another said "he was in a mental state." His female accuser was "in a very drunken state, did not appear to know where she was or what had really transpired. She was unable to identify Doty." Three of the officers describe what they saw inside of Doty's 1951 Pontiac. One observed an electric wire in the trunk. Another describes the wire as about fifty feet of heavy strand, insulated slate gray wire. Another sees small pieces of 20- or 22-gauge single strand wire, the type used to hook up radios and television sets. Two saw a clock, one describes it as two-and-a-half-inch to three-inch in diameter with a white face in a black case. One saw an electric drill and a skill saw. They all saw clothing, shrubbery, and a brown leather briefcase containing papers. And on a front seat a holster for a .22 caliber revolver.[216]

Centerville Square
Noon CT Monday

The offices of Hall Engineering overlook Centerville's courthouse square from the south side. Hall's Chief Engineer/Surveyor, Robert Buss, and his team are entering onto maps the physical details of Flight 11's last path. For five days the team has worked along the forty miles from the Shuey Field crash site to Lake Wapello in Davis County. For two days the team has followed the US Army recruits in their four-wheel-drive jeeps under direction from FBI Director Mark Felt overhead suspended from a helicopter. Robert Buss, with his theodolite, has measured vertical and horizontal axes. Robert's son, Bob, and Ken Boyer have measured the distance of the traverse lines with chains and pins and hold rods for vertical elevation measurement. The team has recorded each numbered lath, the description of each recovered debris marked significant for CAB investigation. Everything . . . all details are recorded into the team's surveyor field notebooks.[218, 219, 220, 221]

Technician Ken Boyer, home from Iowa State University for the summer, is sitting at a large drafting table covered in a mylar polyester sheet. On it he marks the details from the field notebooks. He uses a scale of one-inch to a mile. He draws circles inserting numbers for each lath. They begin with one, two, and three at the crash site to sixty, sixty-one, and sixty-two at Lake Wapello. He enlarges three areas, changing the scale for clarity to one-inch for a quarter mile. These are for the empennage, the engines, and the wings. There are two more maps. One records the profile—the center path of Flight 11's hull onto the Shuey Field. The second gives the topography of the immediate wreckage site, the dotted outline of the craft at the end of its center line. All three maps are blueprinted. The original mylar drawing, the blueprints, and the surveyors' field notebooks are delivered to George Van Epps in the Continental Hotel, a short walk to the square's east side.[217, 222]

Kansas City
2:00 PM CT Monday

After their meeting with the Kansas City, Kansas, police describing the April 23 arrest of Tom Doty, FBI Special Agents Otto Handwerk and Joseph Kelly are crossing the city east to Gillham Plaza in Kansas City, Missouri. At the headquarters of Luzier, Inc, a cosmetics firm, they are meeting with [name redacted], Luzier's head manager for sales. This was Tom Doty's last place of employment. The manager tells the two agents that Doty was hired in July 1961 as a trainee district sales manager. Nine months later, in the first week of April 1962, Doty resigned. And, says the sales manager, "had Doty not resigned he would have been fired." He was unreliable and untrustworthy. He failed to attend assigned sales conferences, lied about having military experience, and lied about having good health.

It was found that Doty was a severe diabetic. Mr. Luzier, the head of the firm, took a business sales trip with Doty "about March 2, 1962" to Atlanta, Georgia. Doty became very ill, was vomiting blood, and the house physician of the Atlanta Biltmore Hotel was called to treat him. At the same time there were rumors. They were about his behavior, about his reputation, about his relationships with women—with Geneva Fraley in particular. He was unable to take instructions, was insubordinate, and felt the job was not good enough for him.[223]

Centerville
3:00 PM CT Monday

At the *Iowegian* office on Main Street south of the Centerville square, Bob Beck and Charlie DePuy have completed this day's edition of the *Centerville Daily Iowegian*. The banner headline in two-and-a-half inch high letters reflects the morning's CAB press conference. It reads: BLAST IS CONFIRMED. Below is Bob Beck's subheading, "Development of Explosion Theory." Bob writes, "While the public originally believed that weather turbulence caused the Boeing 707 to break up in flight last Tuesday night, the experts working on the case didn't ever buy this theory." He quotes George Coffey, the Public Relations officer for Continental Airlines: "Here was a plane that had been tested time and again to withstand several times the strain that could be encountered in known weather conditions." Alongside Bob's article is Charlie DePuy's "Unfolding Drama in Probe." Charlie tracks the evolution of the experts' conclusions at the conference. He ends with three questions: "(1) What kind of explosive force was it? (2) Who did it? (3) And to what justice will the wrong-doer be brought?"[153, 161]

The articles are transmitted from the *Iowegian* to national and world press sources via the *Ottumwa Courier,* the central sending point for Associated Press. The same day the *Courier*—forty-three miles closer to Gayno Smith's crime scenes—sends photographs to the *Iowegian*. There is a family portrait of the murdered McBeth family. At the apex is nineteen-year-old Amos. On either side are his two sisters, Anna, his twin, on his left, and seventeen-year-old Donna on his right. At the base are the parents: Andy (fifty-one) and Dora (forty-two). In the center is fifteen-year-old Patsy Lou, the smallest, the youngest, the only one to survive. With bullet wounds in her shoulder, she escaped to the safety of another farm. It was Patsy Lou who identified Gayno as the killer. There are other photographs—the house where the crime was committed, the barn where two bodies were found, and the Appanoose County sheriff's posse—waiting, searching for Gayno Smith, somewhere in the Udell – Unionville, Iowa, countryside.[224, 225, 228]

"You'd rarely have two major stories that will be front page news copy nationwide breaking at the same time" Bob Gallimore, the *Associated Press* reporter from Kansas City tells Bob Beck. "Centerville has become something of the news capital of the world in the last few days."[229]

Kansas City, Missouri
3:30 PM CT Monday

From the FBI office in the Federal Building on Grand Avenue, twenty-three named FBI special agents and twenty-one more [their names redacted] are radiating across Missouri and Kansas. Their assignment: to learn more about Thomas Gene Doty. They are visiting homes, meeting places, stores, and bars. They are talking to his relatives, his friends, his contacts, those he played poker with, those who worked with him, and those who knew him.[230]

They have obtained his birth certificate. He was born April 17, 1928, in San Antonio, Texas. They've acquired his Kansas City High School and Junior College records from Columbia, Missouri. His University of Missouri records show he was an honor student and member of two professional business fraternities. He studied one year at the Evening School of Law, Kansas City University.

A mixed picture is emerging. For the first thirty-one years of his thirty-four years of life, Doty is described as likeable, optimistic, cheerful, happy, charming, well-groomed, and well mannered. He was able to carry on intelligent, contemporary conversations both in art and in literature where he could quote Shakespeare "by the page." Some others found him "loud," "boisterous," "argumenta-tive," and "boastful," claiming he would be a millionaire before he was forty.

Underlying it all was a serious medical condition.[231]

Kansas City, Missouri, Nichols Road
4:00 PM CT Monday

FBI Special Agent [name redacted] is interviewing Tom Doty's most recent doctor in his office on Nichols Road. The doctor says Doty had been his patient since 1953, when Doty was twenty-five. Doty was referred to him by a doctor who'd known him from childhood but who was now no longer practicing medicine. Doty, the doctor says, was a diabetic—a severe diabetic that warranted daily insulin injections. He was diagnosed when he was sixteen-years of age when Doty's parents were Christian Scientists. Their reaction to his diagnosis, to the years of symptoms of his pre-diabetic condition, is not known. But for the rest of Doty's life, the eighteen years to his death aboard Continental Flight 11, other medical issues persisted. There were urological problems, chronic prostate infections, abdominal pain, nausea, vomiting, diarrhea, shaking, sweating, incoherence, becoming white, staring off into space, weaving and wandering, negative insulin reactions, and coma. He had repeated stays in hospitals in Kansas City and in other cities, too. More than one doctor considered Doty was abusing his health and not living the prescribed life for a diabetic. One referred him for psychiatric evaluation. The psychiatrist, Doty said, had been unable to help him and he corrected the condition himself by reading books on this particular subject. In October 1948 Local Board 51 of the Kansas City Selective Service

System, reading a letter from Dr. Donald Black, Doty's earlier physician, declared Doty 4F.

The physician shows the FBI Agent Doty's records for the years 1960–1961. Doty was in the hospital five times for a total of twenty-three days. There were two stays in June, 1960—for three days and then seven more; in October 1960 for five days; in November 1960 for six days; in April 1961 for two days; and October 16, 1961, the length of stay not given. All these illnesses were caused by diabetes. On one stay he left the hospital against the wishes of the attending hospital physicians and on one occasion he said he wished he was dead.

In April 1962, just before he resigned from Luzier's, he again visited his doctor complaining of diarrhea and nausea. He was then, the doctor reports, on a dosage of insulin: forty units of LENTE and ten units of regular insulin to be taken in the mornings by injection. The doctor also prescribed an antibiotic, an anti-spasmodic medication, and Dramamine, an anti-nausea drug, to ward off air and sea sickness. On May 20, two days before the air crash, Doty phoned requesting a renewal of the prescription of Dramamine.[232]

Unionville, Iowa
4:30 PM CT Monday

All day rumors about Gayno are rife. They arrive to the Unionville, Iowa, headquarters from confusingly multiple directions. A gun shot was heard in the night in the vicinity of the Joe Wilson/Walter Harper farms. Joe Wilson's farm is three miles north of Unionville, Walter Harper's half a mile east of Joe Wilson's. Gayno's been seen in a ditch . . . he's a body dead in a tree (it's a dead limb) . . . he's twenty miles northeast walking toward Ottumwa on the Blue Grass Road . . . he's in a Boy Scout cabin by Lake Wapello . . . he's broken into a house in Moravia ten miles north . . . and into another house two miles east of Ottumwa. Mrs. Earl Tait, at Clarkdale nine miles west, has seen a small tan car, a man emerging from it, changing his clothes, re-entering the car, and now it's heading south on the Mystic Road three miles west of Centerville. Law officers check it out—the tan car is at Stagner's Greenhouse. It belongs to a worker there. Every rumor is checked, but police authorities believe Gayno Smith hasn't gone far. He's still in the Udell/Unionville area. Sheriff Thomas spreads his arms wide indicating the whole area. "He's out there somewhere."[225]

Kansas City, FBI Office
5:00 PM CT Monday

Two times on two previous days—Saturday, May 26, and Sunday, May 27—FBI Special Agent James Glonek has received telephone calls from friends of Passenger #10: Geneva "Jean" Fraley. He checks information on Mrs. Fraley that has already been collected by the FBI. On May 23, the day after the crash, two FBI special agents, Lawrence Larmore and [name redacted], visited Jean Fraley's husband on North Pleasant Street, Independence, Missouri, for routine information about victims. Melvin Fraley supplied a description of his wife: thirty-two-years old, white, height five-foot-five-inches, weight one-hundred-fifteen pounds, brown eyes, blonde hair and with two distinctive scars—one for an appendectomy, the other for the removal of a malignant breast tumor. She is the mother of their two children and has worked for Luzier's since April 1961. This trip to Chicago was the result of a new business she was beginning with Tom Doty and his wife. The following day (May 24), Melvin Fraley was visited again. No police record of his wife Jean Fraley existed, so there is no fingerprint record to aid identifying her at the morgue in Unionville, Missouri. FBI Special Agents Jacob Schmidt and Shea Airey obtain a latent fingerprint from a perfume bottle Mrs. Fraley had used.

Rumors are circulating in Kansas City. They are of a close relationship between Jean Fraley and Tom Doty. Her friends are interviewed.[233]

Kansas City, Gillham Plaza
5:30 PM CT Monday

Special Agent Otto Handwerk returns to Gillham Plaza and interviews [name redacted] who trained both Jean Fraley and Tom Doty for their jobs at Luzier's. Jean Fraley trained for two days in the spring of 1961; Doty for three days in the summer of 1961. The trainer describes Mrs. Fraley as "a very nice appearing business-like woman who during training was very interested in Luzier products." Her experience in training Doty is almost completely redacted. There is one discernable phrase: "Doty appeared to be a very intelligent person."

The same day a second associate, friend [name redacted] of Jean Fraley, is interviewed by a special agent [name redacted]. This friend says she "dearly loved Mrs. Fraley, one of the finest persons she's ever met . . . and the best friend she's ever had." But she "had a dislike for Mr. Doty, which she could not explain but that she had never trusted him."[234]

Kansas City, Private Home (address not given)
6:00 PM CT Monday

The third friend is also interviewed in Kansas City. Both her name and the special agent's name are redacted. This friend of Jean Fraley's gives information that covers seven pages of the FBI official report. She describes Mrs. Fraley as "the most vivacious, dynamic and aggressive personality she had ever known." The friend met Jean and Tom Doty at Luzier's and the three formed a close relationship. The three of them felt some frustration with Luzier's. Their promotional ideas for the company were not listened to. Doty left Luzier's in March 1962, and the three of them became closer. They had lengthy conversations and out of them grew the plans to form their own company. They would call it Gracious Homes. It would be a gift shop as well as supplying objects that would make a home more beautiful. This friend considered Doty "to be a man of exceptional ability as a business executive. He had wonderful ideas and a great personality." He came out with one plan so brilliant that Fraley practically went into ecstasy. They considered hiring others to join—a couple, two interior decorators, one extra woman, and Mrs. Doty was said to be interested too. This friend and Jean Fraley thought this business would begin in the fall of 1962. But Doty had other plans and wanted business underway immediately. On May 17, 1962, the friend, Doty, and Fraley went to the Rialto Building to draw up corporation papers for the new company. He signed a lease for a building on Fairmont Street in Kansas City. Doty made arrangements for the building to be remodeled for an opening day of June 1, 1962.

The next stage was a buying trip to Chicago to acquire merchandise.[235]

Centerville
6:30 PM CT Monday

Boyd O'Briant at the Chamber of Commerce is doing everything possible to find places to stay for all the journalists and reporters covering the Flight 11 crash and the Gayno Smith manhunt. At the telephone exchange, chief operator Mildred Earhart says her office is swamped by calls, "At times the demands for long-distance calls have been higher than could be processed." Local stores are reporting extra sales. Dick Glascock of Centerville Cleaners says the out-of-town demand is unusual. And all eating places are reporting an exceptionally busy time.

Charlie DePuy's workday at the *Iowegian* is completed. He is on his way home. He's anticipating, at last, a good night's sleep. The phone rings. "Hey, there's a guy hiding over there by Unionville, Iowa, who killed his uncle and five members of his family over in Hedrick, Iowa. Better get there."[3]

Tuesday, May 29, 1962

Udell and Unionville, Iowa
9:00 AM CT Tuesday

Night storms with high winds and threatening tornadoes have swept through these wooded hills. Soap Creek and its tributaries are over-flowing. The ground is saturated after four inches of rain. Despite forty-eight hours of searching with more than one-hundred peace officers, there is no sign of Gayno Smith.

A reporter from *Associated Press* and staff writers from the *Centerville Daily Iowegian* are interviewing Sheriff Paul Thomas in Unionville's Legion Hall. He tells them "We really haven't had a good lead since the discovery of the abandoned car . . . No one has seen Smith in the area . . . Each day officers check again with every farmer in the vicinity. This is a hostage precaution." Thomas pauses and then continues, "There's a strong possibility that Smith may be just sitting tight. He may have a good hiding place, and figures it is wise to stay quiet. Food and water will be the thing that will flush him out . . ." There's another pause. The Sheriff continues, "This area is so rough it's impossible to say definitely but I think he has gotten away. I think he's gone. We haven't found any sign of him . . . We are starting to check the possibility that Gayno Gilbert Smith, young farmhand wanted for five killings, may have committed sui-cide . . . his body could be in the area, and would be mighty hard to find in the wooded and timber country . . . it was apparent the boy was having some mental difficulty at the time of the shooting. If he was in the area, he would have been certain to have noticed all the airplanes, cars and search activity. In his confusion, he might just have determined to take his own life. Today we are enlisting the help of all farmers in this area and we are again doing a house to house, building to building probe."[236]

A reporter from the *Bloomfield Democrat* learns Davis County Sheriff Jim Yates, Deputy Larry Morrison, and Highway Patrolman Richard Smith—all of Bloomfield, and with little sleep, are still searching. "They haven't given up that Smith 'a dead-eye shot with a gun and a hunter' is still hiding in the woods if he is alive. The families in this timbered countryside haven't given up either. Some of the homes are without telephones. Bolted doors and loaded fire-arms are within easy reach everywhere."[237]

Centerville
10:00 AM CT Tuesday

Charlie DePuy is back at the *Iowegian* office. He's balancing four major news-breaking stories he has to get onto the front page. The first: the tornadoes that threatened Unionville, Iowa, on Monday night had touched down in neighboring Wayne County extensively damaging farms. The second is the story Charlie himself has just heard at the Continental Hotel. There was a closed meeting there of the CAB, the FBI, the FAA, and Continental Airlines. CAB's Public Relations Officer Edward Slattery emerges to address reporters. He says, ". . . following the conference this morning the CAB is pulling out probably Friday of this week . . . the work of the many officials of the Civil Aeronautics Board is practically complete here. Further investigation lies largely with the FBI . . . the wreckage of the ill-fated jetliner on the Shuey Farm south of the Iowa-Missouri line is being turned over to the Continental Airline insurance company. CAB has agreed to store it for forty-five days if any further reference to it is needed. After that, it and the engines are open to whatever disposition Continental wishes to make of it."

Charlie returns to the *Iowegian* office. He writes his banner headline: FBI HOLDS PARLEY. He subtitles it: CAB LEAVES HERE SOON. As Charlie is writing, a third story breaks on local radio. It's a rumor from Washington DC. A passenger aboard Continental Flight 11 has some court charges against him and is being investigated as having some possible connection with the explosion. Charlie inserts this information inside a box in his mid-column. He labels it "Investigation" and in addition to the story, Charlie, ever the careful newsman qualifies, "The *Associated Press* thru which the *Iowegian* receives its outside news has not reported on this matter thus far. So there seems to be nothing definite of a pin down nature to report." But that was changing as Charlie completed the last sentence . . . It was a fourth news breaking story. This is from Washington DC. And its source: *Associated Press.*[128]

Washington DC
Noon CT Tuesday

In the capitol building in Washington DC, Civil Aeronautics Board chairman, Alan S. Boyd, is appearing before the Senate Aviation Subcommittee. He has received from George Van Epps in Centerville the final conclusion of the cause of the crash of Continental Flight 11. He reports "Investigators found no indication that the crash was the result of any structural defects or anything relating to the aircraft. Shrapnel was found in the body of a hostess who was seated in the rear of the aircraft. A dynamite explosion apparently blew out a side of the plane." In response to a question, he is unable to say whether the blast was from dynamite caps, sticks of dynamite, or something else. He completes his appearance with "The FBI is right on top of this."[128, 238]

Kansas City
1:00 PM CT Tuesday

FBI special agents are, as chairman Alan Boyd describes to the Senate Aviation Subcommittee, "on top of this." "This" being investigating Kansas City area's hardware stores for sales of dynamite. They've been doing it for two days without success. But this is the breakthrough day. It happens to Special Agent Weeter S. Pond and it happens on Leavenworth Road at the Pierce and Tarry Trading Post. The sales clerk tells Agent Pond the firm handles Atlas dynamite and no other brand. The clerk recalls a sale one month to six weeks ago. The customer had been observed in the store on a previous occasion. He was alone. On his second visit, he requested four or six sticks of dynamite, three or four blasting caps, and several feet of orange wax clover safety fuse. The sales clerk said he rolled the fuse and placed it in a brown paper bag together with the sticks of dynamite. The caps he placed in a smaller paper bag and requested the customer place the small bag containing the caps in his shirt pocket and to keep the caps away from the other bag. The sales clerk shows Agent Pond examples of the store's paper bags. One is gray with drawings in white ink of hardware items and the words "Greater Values." A second bag is of brown paper. On the bottom of both of these bags is a flag in red ink and lettering. On the first: "Advance 10, 100% Moleskin," on the second: "Advance 6 100% Kraft Scout." On the third bag, the smallest, the lettering is in blue ink and reads, "Southern Maid, 1, 100% Kraft, SWS." The sales clerk describes the customer: white male, age thirty to thirty-five, height five-foot-ten-inches to five-foot-eleven-inches, weight: one-hundred-seventy-five to one-hundred-eighty pounds, his hair reddish brown and bushy, his complexion fair to medium. Out of nine photographs provided by Agent Pond, the clerk selects the one of Thomas Gene Doty saying he's not "absolutely positive" but "within reasonable certainty" this was the customer.

The co-owner of the Trading Post shows Agent Pond a stick of dynamite in his stock. It is eight inches in length. One-and-one-eighth to one-and-one-quarter inch in diameter. Near one end are the words "Explosives Dangerous." On the side "Extra 40%" and the trademark: Atlas Explosives. The wrapper is waxy and browny-beige in color. The printing is in blue ink. Agent Pond notes that the sales clerk, and the store's co-owner and his wife, all three provide descriptions of Tom Doty prior to seeing the nine photographs. All three independently select the one of Tom Doty before his image has appeared in local Kansas City newspapers.

After a detailed review of the check register, general ledger, paid vouchers, and cash register sales tapes, [name redacted] points to an entry on April 7, 1962. This is for six sticks of dynamite, three blasting caps, and six feet of fuse. The cost was $2.19 + $.05 tax. [Name redacted] expresses the opinion that after his study of the tapes, and computations of possible combinations, he is certain the sale was made to the customer on that date: April 7, 1962.[239]

Kansas City
4:00 PM CT Tuesday

Three special agents: Royal Perkins, Charles Killion, and [name redacted], again with the written consent of Naomi Doty, are searching three vacant homes owned by the Dotys. All three are on streets in Kansas City, Missouri. One is on Virginia, one on Wyandotte and one on Campbell. At the first two there are no items of intrinsic interest. But in the basement of the home on Campbell, a cardboard box is taken for examination. In it are multiple pieces of electrical equipment: plugs, transformers, toggle switches, fluorescent starters, electromagnets, bulb sockets, a switch control box, a rheostat, solder connectors, and seven coils enclosed in porcelain housing.

Hours earlier Special Agent Weeter Pond had established a connection between the store and Doty at the Pierce and Tarry Trading

Post. But there are no bags, receipts, or packing material identifying the Pierce and Tarry Trading Post in any of the three locations.[240]

Unionville, Iowa
6:00 PM CT Tuesday

Evening is approaching for the third night since the murder of the McBeth family. Gayno is still at large. All day there has been no sign of him, but people believe he is hiding somewhere in the area.

Two-and-a-half miles east of Unionville on a rural road (J3T), Dwight Harrington prepares to sleep for the third night downstairs on his sofa, his shotgun close at hand. Upstairs are his wife Jeanne and their three children: Sandy (eight), Barbara (four) and Steve (two). Just east of the Harrington farm, sixty-six-year-old Pete Smith, one of the area's best coon hunters prepares for the night.

Two more Harringtons, John in Unionville and Richard, together with a group of farmers, approach Sheriff Paul Thomas. "We have a plan."[241]

Wednesday, May 30, 1962

Unionville, Iowa
3:30 AM CT Wednesday

If there are any residents of Unionville and Udell who didn't know the Harrington plan to capture Gayno Smith, they know it now. It's 3:30 in the morning and they know it by sound. The plan is for farmers to let their fox hounds out for a hunt. The hounds—lots of them, says Sheriff Paul Thomas—are divided into two groups. Some gather at Gayno Smith's abandoned car and head west. The others head east. The noise—says Sheriff Paul Thomas, waiting with Deputy Sheriff Harry Robertson for developments—is "something awful." The hope is if Gayno can hear the hounds he'll think bloodhounds are on his trail and he'll move. Local pilot Bill Minor is part of the plan. He is ready to fly overhead to see if Gayno makes a move. And Mark Felt, the FBI director of the investigation of Flight 11, is preparing a government helicopter for the same purpose.[242]

East of Unionville, Iowa
5:00 AM CT Wednesday

Two-and-a-half miles east of Unionville, it's the beginning of the farm day for Dwight Harrington. He grasps his shotgun and heads out to check on his animals. It's rained in the night. There's a small abandoned three-room house over on Pete Smith's land. Pete uses it to store oats. This morning it shines wet reflecting the early morning light. The ground is muddy. Pete Smith is moving too. This sixty-six-year-old crosses the road from his farm home and counts his cattle. There are forty-two, not one harmed by the storm in the night. He's crossing back to his house when Pete sees a footprint in the roadway. The sun is rising in the east making visible more footprints, a single set of them heading east. Pete ponders, then goes home to have breakfast. He downs two eggs, two pieces of toast, and tells his wife, "I'm going to follow those tracks wherever they go." Pete follows the trail in his truck. He suspects the footprints belong to Gayno Smith. Pete is unarmed except for an old .22 rifle. Half a mile from his home he sees the footprints start north at a crossroad, "but they make a 'V' and come back, like he isn't sure where he is . . . a stranger around here." Pete's suspicion he's on Gayno Smith's trail becomes stronger.

In another two miles at a second crossroads, Pete sees "Windy" Wendell Bridgeman, his wolf-hunting partner of former days. "I think I'm on that man's trail," Pete tells him. Windy has just completed some milking and is about to take some to his chickens. He leaves the milk in his kitchen and gets into Pete's truck. Pete, experienced in tracking, assesses Gayno's footprints. In front of Pete's house they had been far apart indicating a good pace. But now they are beginning, as Pete says, "to turn out, he is 'plugging,' probably getting tired." Pete and Windy follow the trail three more miles north.[243, 244, 245]

Kansas City
6:30 AM CT Wednesday

FBI Special Agent Alexander P. LeGrand is preparing for another long day in Kansas City libraries. He's responding to Naomi Doty's interview with the FBI at the Federal Building on Sunday, May 27. She said in the fall of 1961 she saw her husband reading books on [redacted]. Agent LeGrand's search reveals the subject: explosives. Mrs. Doty named the three libraries where her husband could have borrowed the books. There is a complication for Agent LeGrand. Mrs. Doty described helping her husband at one of the apartments they rent out and finding a library card with the name of a former tenant. She gave the card to her husband. Special Agent LeGrand will examine library slips of books checked out in more than one name.[246]

The Davis County Line
6:30 AM CT Wednesday

In Pete Smith's truck, Pete and Windy cross the Appanoose/Davis County line and reach the Walter Cantrell farm. Pete asks Walter to notify the authorities. Sheriff Paul Thomas, Deputy Harry Robertson, and three Appanoose officers—Curtis Green, Frank Sconzo, and Dic Tracy—head east from Unionville where they've been based for the night. Davis County Sheriff, Jim Yates, Deputy Larry Morrison, and highway patrol officer Richard Smith head west from Bloomfield. Messages reach two aircraft, Bill Minor's and an FBI helicopter.[242]

6:57 AM CT Wednesday

The footprints continue. They pass the Charles Swaim farm where Pete makes sure the authorities are on their way. The footprints stop at a barn lot gate one mile from Lake Wapello and just north of Adams Cemetery. Pete notes the change in Gayno's footprints, "They're picking up again . . . he's thinking, "I'm going to get some rest now." The barn is on land farmed by Paul Matheny. Paul, conscious that the barn could be a good hiding place for the runaway murderer had found it empty two days ago. He moved sheep that were in that lot a week ago to a new pasture nearer his house.[247]

7:13 AM CT Wednesday

Pete parks his pickup well beyond the barn to prevent arousing Gayno's suspicions. He gets out and maintains a road block to stop traffic from disturbing footprints when approaching Lake Wapello or the Adams Cemetery where visitors will soon be arriving for Memorial Day ceremonies. Windy warns Harold Koop, the supervisor at Lake Wapello, about what is happening. Tom Swaim, just graduated from Davis County High School, arrives with his father Charles. They are both armed. They join Pete and Windy waiting for law officers to arrive. An FBI helicopter and Bill Minor circle overhead. Law officers from both Davis and Appanoose County approach the barn. They see footprints approaching the building and none leaving. Officers shout for Gayno to give up and come out. There is no answer. Inside, the barn's ground level offers no hiding place. There's a six-and-a-half foot ceiling with a haymow above the length and width and a ladder leading to an upper level. On the ladder there is fresh mud. There are more shouts for Smith to give up. There is again no response. Two patrolmen block the north and south windows. Patrolman Richard Smith ascends the ladder supported by Appanoose Deputy Sheriff Harry Robertson. "There he is!" shouts Richard Smith. Gayno is told to lie down on his back with his hands up. He is found behind bales of hay. He offers no resistance. His shotgun rifle, he tells his captors, was stolen from him on Friday the 25th—the day before the five murders. There is no struggle. Gayno is handcuffed and is cooperative as he's led away.[247]

Mrs. Swaim says the captured Smith "looked like the most frightened person I've ever seen." Pete, just for a moment when his eyes meet those of the man he'd helped the law to capture . . . feels sympathy. "And it seemed like he knew I'd helped, although he couldn't have known." Pete is pleased no officer has to shoot the suspect. Gayno's beard growth is light, his clothing dry. He tells officers he found shelter in vacant barns and buildings. Last night, he says he spent in a small abandoned house full of oats. It was early in the morning he saw a farmer across a field emerge from his house to check on his animals. He was carrying a shotgun. To Sheriff Paul Thomas he asks, "Where did they get so many bloodhounds? When I heard them, I had to start moving." What Smith didn't know, says the Sheriff, is they were just fox and coon hounds, and he could have stayed right where he was without fear."[247, 248]

Pete Smith and Windy Bridgeman are praised by the lawmen for their vital role in the capture. Windy hasn't eaten breakfast. He returns home, finishes his chores, puts on his Legion uniform, and goes to Unionville for Memorial Day services. Pete spends the rest of the day yelling answers to national newsmen into the old crank telephone in the kitchen of his home. One of them asks, "You're a Smith—is Gayno a relative?" To which Pete replies, "He ain't no kin of mine—no how."[242, 245]

Kansas City
8:30 AM CT Wednesday

Two libraries named by Mrs. Doty are the Linda Hall on Cherry Street and the Westport Branch of the Kansas City Library on Westport and Wyandotte. At the Linda Hall, Agent LeGrand shows Thomas Doty's photograph. It is not recognized by multiple librarians except for two who describe his appearance as "familiar." One of the two ventures a description: a tall man, taller than her at five-foot-ten-inches and weighing two-hundred pounds. This does not describe Tom Doty. Agent LeGrand learns the Linda Hall is not a lending library. It deals solely with technical and scientific books. The public has access to all material including any on explosives kept in closed stacks. There are four such books in that area: *The Science of High Explosives* by Cook (Monograph Series 139 published by Reinhold 1958); *Cellulose Nitrate* by Miles (Interscience Publishers, Inc. 1955); *Chemistry of Powder and Explosives* by Davis (John Wiley and Sons, Ltd. 1943); and *Explosions, Detonations, Flammability and Ignition* by Mullins and Penner, (Permagon Press, 1959). Special Agent LeGrand under FBI authorization commandeers all four.

At Westport Branch no individual has made an inquiry about books on explosives. No books have been borrowed under the name

Doty. But the library does have one book on the subject. It is *The Chemical Formulary* by Bennett. It is in the volumes: III, IV, and VI (Chemical Publishing Co. in 1936, 1939, and 1943.) Agent LeGrand commandeers all three.[246]

Sigourney, Iowa
9:00 AM CT Wednesday

Gayno has arrived at the Keokuk County Jail in Sigourney. He is waiting for a murder charge from Justice of the Peace Tom Johnston. He tells Keokuk County Sheriff John Wallerich the McBeth family was still alive early Sunday when he left to visit his mother in Denver, Colorado. He stopped along the road to sleep and awoke to hear a broadcast of the killings, listing him as the suspect. He took off, he says, in rough country to work his way back to Sigourney to tell his story to the Sheriff.[247, 248]

9:15 AM CT Wednesday

Sixteen miles away in Hedrick the high school gymnasium is being prepared for the mass funeral of the five members of the McBeth family. Six-hundred people are attending. Sheriff Wallerich offers Gayno the opportunity to attend the funeral under armed guard. Gayno declines. The Sheriff asks him where is the combination shotgun/rifle? Gayno doesn't answer. Sheriff Wallerich contacts Sheriff Thomas in Appanoose County for help. The gun used for the murders will provide crucial evidence.[202, 247]

Kansas City
1:00 PM CT Wednesday

Mrs. Doty's third named library is the Johnson County Library on Wyandotte and Highway 50. Librarians looking at Tom Doty's photograph do not know him and do not recall him from the library. There has been one request for a book on explosives. One librarian [name redacted] recalls such an inquiry. She obtained it for one customer [name redacted, telephone number given] and ordered *Pyrotechnist's Treasury* by Thomas Kentish from Brigham Young University via Interlibrary loan on September 20, 1961. The book was returned to the library and to Brigham Young University on October 26, 1961. She states the book contained information on fireworks. The same individual on the same day, October 26, 1961, requested a book *Chemistry of Powder and Explosive* by Wiley. It was requested from the Kansas City Public Library on October 26, 1961, but it was never received. The Librarian says that the only way to determine what books an individual has drawn from the library is to examine every withdrawal slip made at the library. Four-thousand to five-thousand are issued every week. Reviewing slips extending from the due date August 26, 1961 through books due June 9, 1962 is now what special agent LeGrand is doing. It takes him five days with assistance from six other agents [all names redacted]. The work reveals Mrs. Doty and [name redacted] at the same address, checked out children's books. Thomas Doty drew out one book, *Dianetics*. Agent LeGrand withdraws it from the library along with *The Illustrated Encyclopedia of Science and Technology* by Editors of Unified Encyclopedia (Stuttmans 1961); and volumes four, five and ten of McGraw Hill Encyclopedia of Science and Technology (McGraw Hill 1960).[246]

Kansas City Airport
4:00 PM CT Wednesday

The books removed from three Kansas City libraries by LeGrand are being prepared for shipment at the Kansas City Airport. They are the four books from Linda Hall, the three from the Westport Branch, and the five from Johnson County Library. These will be flown by air express to the Single Fingerprint Laboratory in Washington DC. They will be examined for latent fingerprints and, any found, compared with those of Thomas Doty.[246]

Thursday, May 31, 1962

Centerville
9:00 AM CT Thursday

The departure of the CAB team from Centerville is imminent. At the Continental Hotel, Lead Investigator George Van Epps and Public Relations Coordinator Edward Slattery are holding their last press conference. Charlie DePuy and *Centerville Daily Iowegian's* Editor Bob Beck are present. So are *AP*, local, state, and national reporters. George Van Epps begins by expressing his sincere thanks "to the people in this area for the wonderful help they have extended." "95%" he says, "of the aircraft parts have been recovered . . . hundreds of people brought things to their local police on a voluntary basis." Edward Slattery extends gratitude, "Please express my appreciation to the people of Centerville, Unionville, Missouri, and farmers and people in other communities in this area. The cooperation has been wonderful . . . no farmer resented the helicopter landing in his field. There hasn't been one unpleasant thing insofar as the relationship between our people and the folks in the area. I say this, because it's not always the case."

Questions are directed to the two men from the press. Van Epps responds that the CAB suspected in twenty-four hours that an explosion was caused by a bomb. "By Friday morning, the evidence was very strong. Everything since has simply reinforced this explosion finding." Slattery cites the evidence: "1) the lack of indication of an air load on the tail section which was perfectly flat when found. If it had been broken apart by air turbulence, it would have been bent or wrinkled. 2) The fact two-hundred-twenty inches of the fuselage was missing, which would not have been the case if the plane broke up because of turbulence and 3) The manner in which the metal skin of the plane was curled, which indicated an explosive force."

Slattery intends recommending some sort of recording device for a pilot. "Captain Gray did not communicate . . . he could have been too busy . . . but he was probably alive for a minute and a half at least." Van Epps makes a pronouncement, "There have been three previous cases in which an engine powered airplane was destroyed by a bomb in the United States . . . the crash of this Continental Airlines jet May 22 will make aviation history. We are leaving the investigation in the hands of the FBI."

There's an exchange from Edward Slattery to Charlie DePuy, "Just the minute our investigation and summary are complete I will send you a complete report."[249, 250, 251]

Shawnee, Kansas
10:00 AM CT Thursday

In Shawnee, Kansas, two agents [both names redacted] are searching a 1958 four-door Biscayne, white over green Chevrolet. It was traded by Doty three days prior to his death and is currently in the Ray Klein Body Shop on Johnson Drive. They are finding much discarded material. The two agents remove two bags of debris for "evidentiary purposes." One of the bags is from a vacuum cleaner. There are multiple pieces of baling wire, plastic tubing, rubber covered cord, one piece of grass rope, sale slips, a cloth, a twelve-inch ruler, half of a metal box labeled "Herb-Ox" and a small wooden paddle labeled "Mautz Rubber Satin." There's no container for the "Rubber Satin." They find it floating upside down in a stream at Antioch Park in Merriam. Mrs. Doty says she threw it there on May 26, 1962. That was four days after the airplane crash. If she offers an explanation, it is not cited.[343]

Centerville
Noon CT Thursday

In the *Centerville Daily Iowegian* office on North Main Street just off the Square, Editor Bob Beck, for days, has been struggling with his editorials. There is so much to say. So much that is emotional for this man. He writes, "One cannot appreciate the depth and the scope of the investigation until he has seen it at close range." And Bob has seen it. He's watched it. He's heard it. He lists "every kind of a top expert" studying at the crash site and staying at the Continental Hotel. "The weather people . . . the FAA authorities establishing the flight line and pattern. The Civil Aeronautics Board is in charge of the over-all investigation. But they have a world of assistance: Boeing Aircraft specialists, Pratt and Whitney engine manufacturers, metal, hydraulic, electrical experts, and now the FBI . . . Whenever an air disaster occurs," he tells his readers, "you can rest assured that everything possible is going to be done to determine the cause." Bob has flown on 707 jets on numerous occasions. He finds the 707 "a wonderful airplane." But if sabotage is the cause of this crash, Bob supports George Van Epps who wants voice recorders installed for pilots. Bob adds, "More stringent baggage inspection will be necessary."[253]

   In today's editorial Bob's appreciation is to his staff. "The *Iowegian* has never been called upon to handle two major stories of nationwide magnitude all in the same day. This happened in our last Monday and Tuesday issues when the airplane crash story was reaching a crescendo and the manhunt was well underway." Then the newspaper needed help and it got it. Bob lists everyone in all phases of the newspaper's operation right down to the carriers delivering the newspaper to the streets. He also thanks *The Ottumwa Courier* which cooperated with pictures. Edward Slattery CAB's Public Relations Coordinator, he says, "patiently explained everything to the press." Louis Ver Baere, in charge of engraving, "had to really apply the steam." And the Managing Editor? Charlie DePuy? He "was practically on an around the clock basis."[125]

Kansas City, Missouri
2:00 PM CT Thursday

Special Agents Leon Lake Jr. and Nellis Manson have the assignment of learning Doty's business history. They are meeting with Frederick T. Reyling. He said he met Doty years ago in a group poker game. Between 1943 and 1957, Doty held miscellaneous employments. But on April 17, 1957, Doty's twenty-ninth birthday, he became president of his own company. He named it Associated Research Products Company, Inc. for the manufacture and sale of fiberglass burial vaults. He acquired a building on Southwest Boulevard in Kansas City and Frederick Reyling became the secretary/treasurer. Despite Doty's diabetic condition, Reyling says, he worked seven days a week showing great drive and, when discouraged, would quickly recover, become creative, and proceed with his patents. Dun and Bradstreet (the provider of national business data), reflected the business volume of Associated Research Products "increasing substantially and operations reportedly profitable." That was on July 7, 1960. It was two months out of date. On April 23 a fire loss at the business cost Doty $17,000 and worse, what he believed to be his patents and his copyrights were forfeited to Newcomer's Funeral Home. This loss deeply affected Doty. "It shook him up real bad," said Reyling. Doty was thirty-two-years-old and without a job.[254]

Fairway, Kansas
3:00 PM CT Thursday

Another Doty car is being searched. Two FBI special agents, Royal Perkins and [name redacted] are in the Methodist parking lot at Fairway, Kansas, with a 1951 Pontiac. Again the search yields possible evidentiary material: receipts, brake guarantees, an empty box that once held a Power Kraft circular saw blade, letters, contracts, and sales slips, including two from Kansas City hardware stores. These stores were Brogoto on Prospect and Bunting on Walnut. But no sales slip or packing bag from Pierce and Tarry is discovered. They also find two pairs of trousers and one waist-length jacket.[255]

The Crash Site
5:00 PM CT Thursday

Charlie DePuy is arriving at the crash site "for one last picture." He finds the place strangely quiet. There are no guards at the highway leading to the Shuey farm. There are no guards at the road leading to the crash site. Under a big tree near the fuselage there are two soldiers from Fort Leonard Wood. They tell Charlie "Interest has practically died down and the sightseers and curious have quit coming to the scene." Phone lines to the site have been disconnected. Clarence Stillwagon of the CAB is in charge of "the mop up." He's in Centerville still accepting plane parts from people and the police stations. But he knows, as Edward Slattery has said, 95% of the plane has been recovered. The mock-up of the tail section in a building at the Appanoose County Fairgrounds is under lock and key. Appanoose Fair Secretary Carl Robey asks CAB officials if the mock-up might be an exhibit for when the Appanoose County Fair opens on July 30. He's told no. The mock-up will be moved out on July 15 and taken to an FAA school near Oklahoma City. Most of the news media personnel have left. John Ratterman of the *Kansas City Star* is still in town. *Life* magazine has two people working on an artistic reproduction of the accident with an artist from New York. Charlie climbs up the hill past the fuselage and takes his picture. It's of empty airline seats set out in two rows on the hill just as they were in the cabin of Flight 11. Charlie writes: "Forty-five persons sat in those seats, one of them with the knowledge that the trip would end in death. The others thought about their work, their plans, their homes. Then there was an explosion and a crippled ship spewing parts over the countryside and finally falling to its death. Now nine days later the story comes to an end." Charlie captions the photograph in the *Centerville Daily Iowegian*, "At the time this picture was taken threatening clouds hovered as they did on the night of the fatal crash."[256, 257, 258]

June 1962

Udell, Iowa
Friday, June 1, 1962, 10:39 AM CT

Beginning at Glenn Cridlebaugh's land north of Udell, Appanoose County Sheriff Paul Thomas is "backtracking." He's following the route taken by Gayno Smith on his three-day escape through Appanoose and Davis Counties. Sheriff Thomas says he's worked out the route Smith took eluding capture. The sheriff is looking for anything Smith might have lost or abandoned. He's looking in empty barns and in abandoned huts. He's looking amid piles of shelled corn and oats in the small abandoned house on Pete Smith's land. Purses and billfolds belonging to the five McBeth family victims are missing. "And," says Sheriff Thomas, "we want especially to find the under-and-over gun which we believe he used to kill five people with."[77, 247, 351]

Sigourney, Iowa
Friday, June 1, 1962, Noon CT

Sixty-seven miles to the north and northeast in Sigourney, the county seat of Keokuk County, Gayno Smith is appearing before Justice of the Peace T.K. Johnson. He pleads "not guilty" to five counts of murder. Sheriff Wallerich says Smith's signed statement conflicts with the one given by fifteen-year-old Patsy Lou McBeth, the only one to escape from the farmhouse near Martinsburg last Saturday. Patsy Lou, with bullet wounds in her shoulder, said Smith did the shooting.[247, 339]

Merriam, Kansas
Friday, June 1, 1962, 2:00 PM CT

Two special agents, Royal M. Perkins and [name redacted] are arriving at the home of Naomi Doty on West 71st Terrace. They come at her specific invitation. She tells them she has "thought and thought" about the information she is about to relay. She does so because it "might have some possible connection with this investigation." She tells it in two parts. First, she reviews what she saw in her husband's briefcase in the trunk of their 1951 Pontiac. It is heavily redacted in the FBI report. Second, she recalls her husband telephoning her from [redacted] Kansas City, Kansas, and advising her of [redacted]. This, presumably, is the arrest of her husband in Kansas City, Kansas, on April 23, 1962. The following day she collected him and they returned home. It was later that day, at 5:00 PM, the two discussed what had happened the night before. She says her husband was upset. She was crying. She told her husband the possibility the information would appear in newspapers. Children in the neighborhood would learn it and result in their daughter being teased. In response her husband said that before he would let this happen [words are redacted]."*340*

Centerville
Friday, June 1, 1962, 11:00 AM CT

Bob Beck, the editor of the *Centerville Daily Iowegian,* is consumed by the two major stories in the area—the air crash and the manhunt. He begins his "Weekend Special, Publisher's Corner" with a promise to return to "our more standard column format" in today's edition. But today it's the air crash. He meets Leo Craver and tells again how Leo, with Jack Morris on the night of May 22, found the first piece of wreckage.

Leo and Barbara Craver and Jack and Judy Morris had taken a drive to Unionville. They had a sandwich, drove around Unionville, looked at some new houses, and started home. Leo observed, "What a beautiful clear night." Between the old and new Exline cutoffs a few minutes south of Centerville they noticed something out in the road. They had to drive wide to miss it . . . They went back to look at it. It was a piece of aluminum about three feet long and six inches wide. They examined it carefully in the car headlights and thought maybe it was a part from a light airplane. It was 9:30 PM, Leo thought. This was within minutes of the explosion. Leo said, "Should we take this to the police station?" Leo and Jack were hesitant. "If we tell them we think a plane is down, they'll think we're nuts." Leo recalls saying. But they decided to show the police. Sheriff Paul Thomas was called. He thought they ought to take a closer look, so Jack, Leo, and the sheriff drove back to the place where they found the first piece. At this time, no one knew a thing about a missing airliner. Word had not reached the local authorities. Soon, Iowa state patrolman Willard Pickard and Sgt. Jimmy Douglas arrived. Leo said he wondered for a time if this wasn't something that had been lost by a truck, and maybe a lot of fuss was being made about nothing. Then they got to searching out in the fields on each side of the road and kept finding pieces. Leo said he knew then it wasn't something that had fallen off a truck. But no one realized that a big plane had crashed. The first indication of that was the discovery of a piece of paper that said something to the effect that it was Continental Airlines and gave a seat number. This was the tip-off that a major plane crash had occurred. The search moved to Cincinnati, and by this time the crowd was growing. Confirmation had been received that an airliner was down. From Cincinnati the search just kept moving to the southwest. At 3:30 AM the search just seemed to stop. They were at the state line, and coffee was being served. Most people had been up all night looking. Also, people realized that dawn was only a short time away, and that the plane would be found in daylight.

Bob Beck continues, Leo was one of the first, along with Milton Kruzich, to reach the scene of the accident. Leo says he had a strange reaction as the wreckage first came into view. "It was the prettiest spring morning imaginable. The birds were singing. Everything seemed so peaceful. And there was the wreckage, all still and serene, sitting in the middle of an alfalfa field. Yet I knew in that plane there was death. I knew what to expect. It was a funny feeling." One of the odd sidelights was that Leo was wearing a good suit that night. The next morning it was torn and muddy. But it was a night long to remember. Bob finishes his column: "Leo's story is just one of hundreds that could be told about the airline crash. It will go down in local history as one of the greatest stories of all time."[341]

Kansas City Airport
Friday, June 1, 1962, Noon CT

Special agents from the Kansas City Office are submitting items to the FBI Laboratory in Washington DC for testing. These are: 1) debris, possibly broken glass, found in the black plastic purse of Geneva Fraley. Mrs. Fraley is Passenger #10, Tom Doty's business associate in their new business, Gracious Homes, Inc. and 2) the glass jar recovered from a stream in Antioch Park, Johnson County, Kansas.[342]

Airport: Kansas City
Saturday, June 2, 1962, Noon CT

More items are being sent to the Washington DC FBI Laboratory from Kansas City. They include items recovered from the trunk of the 1951 Pontiac: 1) a waist-length jacket, 2) two pairs of trousers, 3) a pair of canvas shoes, 4) seven keys from land near Udell, Iowa, discovered in the pocket of a portion of a man's black jacket, 5) the same man's black jacket and, 6) the briefcase bearing the initials TGD found by Gabe Raskie near Cincinnati, Iowa, already sent to the Chicago division is forwarded on to Washington DC for more testing.[252]

Kansas City, Missouri
Saturday, June 2, 1962

At the FBI office in the federal building on Grand Avenue, Special Agent James Glonek is assembling the FBI official report. Other agents are still making calls discovering more about Thomas Doty and over the next days they submit their reports. Special Agents Joseph Kelly and Otto Handwerk are seeking information on Doty's drinking patterns. They are visiting local taverns and bars. The managers at The Keg on Main Street, the Old Heidelberg on South Main, the Red Head Inn on Broadway, and the Drag-Inn on South Troost do not recognize Doty from photographs the agents present. The manager [name redacted] at Joe's Flood Room on Southwest Boulevard does. He says Doty was a customer three or four years ago when he was the proprietor of a burial vault company half a block north of his tavern. He says Doty had a good reputation until fire destroyed his business. Occasionally Doty would come in and drink excessively but never to the extent of becoming obnoxious. There is nothing he knows which would reflect adversely on Doty's character and integrity. But his words reveal a pattern.*344*

From the date of that fire at his business in August 1960, Doty's life begins a downward spiral. In February 1962 he filed voluntary bankruptcy. By April—poet T.S. Eliot's "Cruelest Month"—Doty is ordered by bankruptcy court to turn over his patents and assets. He suffers severe mental depression. The downward spiral accelerates. That same month, April 1962, in the first week, he resigns from Luzier's—leaving voluntarily before he is fired. On April 7 he buys dynamite at Pierce and Tarry Hardware Store. On April 12 it is his thirty-fourth birthday, perhaps providing a reminder that on the same day in 1957, he was CEO of his own company. Now he is bankrupt. He has six years left to become the millionaire he promised himself. On April 23 he is arrested in Kansas City, Kansas. On April 26 his business patents and copyrights business are forfeited.

The next month, May 16, six days before the crash of Flight 11, one of Doty's tenants sees Doty, usually "a happy, charming, well-mannered person," walking to his car on Gillham Road. He appeared "very tired and walked in a slumped manner as if it pained him to walk." That same week or the following one, another tenant of Doty's who lives on the top floor, sees Doty drunk behind the apartment house. Despite this, Doty appears full of plans for the new business, Gracious Homes, he is creating with Jean Fraley. On May 17 the two of them are at the office of an attorney in Kansas City's Rialto Building. They are signing papers to make their business a corporation. Doty leases a building on Fairmont Street and contacts a building company for alterations making the building ready for the start of business on June 1, 1962.

On May 18, together with his wife Naomi and their small daughter, Doty buys a 1962 Ford Fairlane "500" at the Mission Ford in Mission, Kansas. Doty asks the salesman [name redacted] if the company sells credit life insurance. The salesman tells him it's available at the Ford Company credit office in Kansas City, Missouri. Doty then asks when this would take effect. Doty asks twice. The salesman, curious, asks why Doty was so interested in this. Doty replies that he has sugar diabetes and could "go at any time." Doty also asks the salesman if he is sure if anything happened to him (Doty) "within the next two or three days" would his wife receive the car free and clear? The salesman assures Doty she would.

It is the next day, May 19, three days before the crash, that Doty is booking two airline tickets, one for himself and one for Jean Fraley. They are for a flight to Chicago by TWA Flight 122 leaving Kansas City at 6:50 AM on May 21. He also buys two tickets on Continental Flight 11 for May 22, 1962. An original reservation to return to Kansas City on TWA 139 on May 23 is cancelled in favor of the earlier return, Continental Flight 11, the fatal trip back to Kansas City.

The Iowa/Missouri Borderland
Monday, June 4, 1962

The news came first on Sunday, June 3, by radio. Air France Flight 007, a Boeing 707 luxury jetliner, crashes at Orly Airport in Paris. One-hundred-thirty-three were aboard. One-hundred-thirty are dead and most are Americans.[345]

People are waiting for today's *Centerville Daily Iowegian* to read the details. They come from Paris, from Rodney Angove for Associated Press. He writes that eye witnesses reported the Air France aircraft rose a few feet then plunged to the ground, thundered down Runway 8, raced wildly over a rolling wooded slope, burst into flames, and stopped short of homes in the ancient village of Villeneuve du Roi. Two Air France hostesses seated in the tail section were flung to safety and survived. A steward was pulled out alive but died later in hospital. All the passengers were American and most were from Atlanta, Georgia. One-hundred-six of them were members of the Atlanta Art Association on their way home after a three-week tour of European art galleries and cultural sites. Mayor Ivan Allen of Atlanta flies immediately, on another 707, to inspect the scene, to help identify bodies, many of them Atlanta's cultural leaders, and arrange for their transportation home.[346, 349]

World and national attention is beginning to shift away from Putnam and Appanoose Counties. It's becoming "fly-over" country again. These people here with their fortitude, their courage, their instant response to the event, and their unfailing kindness are being overlooked and almost forgotten. But not quite.[347]

"134 Die in Weekend Plane Crashes" is the *Daily Iowegian's* headline about the Paris crash. Just below, dominating the upper half of the paper's front page are two portrait photographs. They measure six inches by three inches. One is Mrs. Geneva Fraley, the other Thomas Gene Doty. Suddenly the speculation, the innuendo is turning into titillating gossip.[259]

Kansas City
Tuesday, June 5, 1962

The gossip of an intimate personal relationship between Jean Fraley and Tom Doty is already in circulation. In Washington DC, Alan S. Boyd, chairman of the CAB, is pursued by the press. He says he cannot comment on reports that a "love triangle" was involved, but "The FBI has the responsibility for determining motives." For the FBI investigators in Kansas City, the nature of the relationship is critical. Was Mrs. Fraley a party to a bomb plot? The FBI interviews with Jean Fraley's close friends probing this issue are heavily redacted. So are those with Melvin Fraley, Jean Fraley's husband. In one of Mr. Fraley's interviews at the federal courthouse building, he tells Special Agent Nicholas Lore that he is "terribly upset" by the publicity inferring his wife and Doty [redacted]. This is nothing but "malicious and barefaced lies." He would swear on a stack of bibles that [redacted]. [166, 260, 261]

Mr. Fraley gives an account of the morning of May 21. When Jean Fraley left her home in Independence, Missouri, for her flight to Chicago she, as always, looked polished and professional. She was wearing a dark blue suit, black shoes, white hat and gloves, and a string of pearls. The plan, her husband understood, was that the Dotys, Tom and Naomi, were driving to Chicago. There they'd meet a couple interested in the new business and one female associate. Jean Fraley would meet all five of them there on May 21. Her ticket was for TWA Flight 122 departing Kansas City at 6:50 AM. She drove herself to the airport, leaving her car there so she could drive home in it on the night of May 22. [261]

On the same morning from Merriam, Kansas, Naomi Doty drove her husband to the airport to catch the same flight, TWA 122. Mrs. Doty, seven-and-a-half months pregnant, had withdrawn from driving to Chicago on the advice of her doctor. She waited in the car with their five-year-old daughter. Her husband brought her an insurance plan and said he planned to stay at the Sherman House

Hotel. Later in the morning Naomi Doty drove their four-day-old 1962 Ford Fairlane "500" to the Mission Ford Company for servicing. When the salesman drove Mrs. Doty and her young daughter home, the daughter said, "I'll bet you don't know where my Daddy is—he's in Chicago looking for a job." At this point the salesman told the FBI that Mrs. Doty told her daughter "to shut up."[263]

On the evening of May 22, Melvin Fraley was on shift work at his place of employment beginning at 4:00 PM and normally finishing at 12:30 AM. At 11:00 PM he hadn't received the usual call from his wife telling him that she was home. And on the radio he heard a Chicago to Kansas City aircraft was lost or crashed. He drove immediately to the Continental Airlines ticket counter at the Kansas City Municipal Airport. At approximately 2:30 AM on May 23 he was shown a passenger list. He read that Mrs. Geneva Fraley was on this list and so was a T. Doty. This was Melvin Fraley's first indication that Tom Doty had not traveled to Chicago by private automobile. He couldn't understand why his wife and Doty were on the same plane. Perhaps Mrs. Doty, "expecting any day," might have changed her plans to go to Chicago by car.[261]

In Merriam, Kansas, it was Wednesday morning when neighbors of Mrs. Doty noted in the newspaper a T. Doty was listed as a passenger on the crashed Continental Flight 11. They went to the Doty home to offer help. Mrs. Doty did not indicate she was aware her husband's name was on the passenger list. She said she didn't expect him home until Wednesday night, the May 24, and he was staying at the Sherman. The couple phoned the long-distance operator at the Sherman. No Doty was presently at the Sherman or the nearby Essex, but the Essex House Hotel had a Doty registered there one or two days prior.

The same neighbors next contacted Continental Airlines at 10:00 AM or 11:00 AM on May 23. Tom Doty was indeed a passenger on Continental Flight 11. When the husband gave this news to Mrs.

Doty, "Mrs. Doty did not appear to take the news too hard and [did] not break into tears. The wife felt Naomi Doty was in a state of mental shock. She did not show much outward emotionalism. She just could not believe her husband was dead."[264]

Kansas City / The Nation
Tuesday, June 5, 1962

No denial by Mr. Fraley can halt the gossip. It continues to build. FBI agents in Chicago, alert to Tom Doty's multiple insurance coverages, had tracked his stay at the Sherman House Hotel the night before the crash. Their report had been written on May 23.

> Mr. and Mrs. T. DOTY, whose photographs were not identified, registered at the Sherman House, Chicago, Illinois, May 21, 1962 at 10:10 AM in Room 1669, and checked out May 22, 1962 at 5:58 PM. On May 21 and 22, 1962, both FRALEY and DOTY were positively identified through photographs as having visited gift shops in the Merchandise Mart, Chicago, Illinois, where they placed orders for merchandise. Both were also positively identified by witnesses as boarding Continental Airline Flight Number 11, about 9:25 PM [sic], on May 22, 1962, at the O'Hare International Airport, Chicago, Illinois, and DOTY was identified as carrying a bulky briefcase subsequently identified by witnesses after it was recovered from the wreck. Both had purchased $75,000 flight insurance at the Airport Sales Company, Chicago, Illinois.[262]

But on that night, Monday, May 21, 1962, there are three curious midnight telephone calls from Chicago to Jean Fraley's three closest friends back in Kansas City.

The first, [name redacted] said she did not go to the plane with Jean but spent the weekend at a resort at Lake of the Ozarks. She usually returns to Kansas City early Monday morning. This weekend she delayed one day. Both Tom Doty and Jean Fraley had tried to call her at midnight. Any message that occurred is redacted.[265]

A second friend of Mrs. Jean Fraley meets FBI Special Agent James Glonek at the Howard Johnson Restaurant in Independence, Missouri. On that night of May 21, she tells, she and her new husband were not at their residence but at their lake summer home. When they returned they were told by their housekeeper, Naom Jones, who is known to both Fraley and Doty, that Doty called about midnight. He asked for the friend but was told she was not available. Doty then said something to the effect [redacted]. Naom Jones assumed it was just another of Doty's jokes.[266]

There was a third call from Doty on the night of May 21. This is to a third friend. Doty told her he had lost Jean. She responded that he was kidding her. He again said, "I am not. I have lost Jean."[267]

Udell/Unionville, Iowa
Wednesday, June 6, 1962

It's been a week since the capture of Gayno Gilbert Smith. From Udell to Unionville to the barn near Lake Wapello where Gayno was caught, the hunt is on for Gayno's over-under-gun, the one used in his murders. For Appanoose Sheriff Paul Thomas, Deputy Harry Robertson, and local officers, the search has been futile. Today Sheriff Thomas attempts another tactic. He collects Gayno from the Sigourney jail. He drives him along the route where Gayno ran and hid. He questions him: Where did he throw that gun? Gayno answers with half-truths, part confession, and outright lies. He seems to feel, says Sheriff Thomas, "that as long as the gun was not found he had a chance to avert a murder sentence."[268]

In Sigourney, Keokuk County Sheriff John Wallerich says Gayno Smith has admitted to the killing of his uncle and aunt and three cousins . . . "he has admitted it to me orally . . . But he has not given us a written confession. In questioning him, he gave no reason.

That's still a mystery." Smith faces five charges of murder. There'll soon be a sixth.[268]

Hedrick, Iowa
Wednesday, June 13, 1962

No one in Hedrick has seen Gayno Smith's stepmother since October. "She said something about going to California," says Gayno from Sigourney jail. Mrs. Juanita Smith is forty-five years old. Her nude body, encrusted with lime, is found in a three-foot hole near a shed on the back of the lot right outside her east bedroom window. There is a cupid tattoo on her left shoulder. An attorney representing Gayno Smith on murder charges in the slaying of five members of the Andrew McBeth family breaks the news to Gayno. "I didn't do it." is Gayno's response. "I don't care whether he admits it or not" said Sheriff John Wallerich. "We've got plenty of evidence to convict him."[269, 270, 271, 272, 273]

The Crash Site
Wednesday, June 13, 1962

By mid-June 1962 crews begin clearing the remains of Continental Flight 11 from the Shuey Field. The overall work is handled by the Haggard Heavy Hauling Company of Kansas City, Missouri. The personal items—the suitcases, the loose clothes, the shoes, had been already moved by the Kansas City FAA team working with head of the FAA, Najeeb Halaby. They were taken to the end room of the Appanoose County fairgrounds building in Centerville. That's where thirteen-year-old Nancy Niday (Roberts) saw them and was disturbed at the sight.[5, 198]

Items are removed from the aircraft's cargo section: boxes of Spanish textbooks, cases of women's bathing suits, and in a rumor that reaches eight-year-old Robert Fowler in Unionville, the broken parts of a possible dog crate. The Durbin Corporation, a scrap metal dealer, purchases the plane's aluminum wreckage. In five railroad cars it is hauled to Kansas City and to Omaha, Nebraska, where it is melted down into ingots and made into lawnmowers.[66]

Lavan Smith, an excavating contractor in Unionville, is hired by Continental Airlines to recover Flight 11's four, fifteen-foot-long Pratt and Whitney JT3C-6 engines. They had torn away from the aircraft and followed their own southwest trajectories, slamming deep into the ground on the Bill Bernecker farm one-and-one-eighth miles ahead of the main fuselage. "Loading these wasn't really difficult," says Lavan, "I loaded them onto a low-bed semi-trailer."[274, 275, 276]

Don Shuey is paid compensation by Continental's insurance company for his losses including damages caused by jet fuel saturating some five acres, ruining that land for crops for five years. Don plowed the crash area to a depth of sixteen inches to prevent livestock from picking up small bits of metal. He put "Keep Out" signs around the land, but Don told Duane Crawford that on July 8, just five weeks after that crash, about fifty cars came to the area. They brought sightseers carrying shovels so they could dig for souvenirs.[66]

Kansas City, Missouri
Thursday, June 14, 1962

At the Kansas City FBI office in the federal building on Grand Avenue, Special Agent James F. Glonek attaches his name to form 263 and releases the bureau's official investigation report into the crash of Continental Airline's Flight 11. It's transmitted to Bureau Chief J. Edgar Hoover at the FBI headquarters in Washington DC. Copies go to division offices in Chicago, Denver, Omaha, and to the Civil Aeronautics Board. It is a major contribution to the CAB's Report, still being prepared, and due out in August.[277]

Pages one and two provide Glonek's summary of the eight-hundred-page report. It is titled: "Investigation Regarding Thomas

Gene Doty, Passenger Number 9, and Geneva Opal Fraley, Passenger Number 10." On the second page are the redacted words of Naomi Doty given on June 1 at her home to Special Agents Royal Perkins and [name redacted]. Mrs. Doty reveals her husband's response to the family's embarrassment resulting from his arrest in Kansas City, Kansas, on April 23, 1962. She quotes her husband saying before he would let any embarrassment occur, "he would do away with himself" in a way which would appear accidental. Mrs. Doty continues in the summary: ". . . she believed her husband might have been responsible for [the] airplane crash. She explained he had told her he was reading in [the] library regarding explosives in the fall of 1961 and four to six weeks before the crash, she saw in his car, objects which she thought were explosives."[278]

Throughout the report and at the end, the FBI laboratory in Washington DC gives the results for items submitted for examinations:

> Residue on a piece of twisted aluminum from the aircraft's "right aft lavatory electrical junction box cover" is consistent with and typical of . . . that remaining after the detonation of dynamite.[279]

> The eleven books sent from the Linda Hall Library, the Johnson County Library, and the Westport Branch of the Kansas City, Missouri, library were examined with iodine fumes. No latent fingerprints of value were developed.[280]

> No significant residue of debris was found inside Doty's briefcase found by Gabe Raskie on land a mile east of Cincinnati or inside Mrs. Fraley's purse. Doty's coat, his keys, items and clothing recovered from his 1951 Pontiac were equally free.[281]

> The small piece of waxy beigy-brown paper found at the crash site and in the arm of hostess Martha Joyce Rush identified as the wrapping of Atlas dynamite is inconclusive.

The letters are black. But the makers of Atlas dynamite—the Atlas Company Explosives Division in Wilmington, Delaware, state it has placed only blue lettering on its products for 40 years. And the lettering on their Atlas wrappings reads "Explosives Dangerous" not "Danger" as seen by Mrs. Doty on those in the car.[281]

Much as the link between the small beigy-brown paper and Atlas dynamite is inconclusive, so is the evidence against Thomas Doty. It was what is declared as "inconclusive." There was no evidence of a suicide pact between Doty and Mrs. Fraley. . . it is believed she had no knowledge of his intentions.[166, 283]

August 1962

Centerville, Iowa
Wednesday, August 1, 1962

From Washington DC, the Civil Aeronautics Board releases the Official Accident Report of Continental Flight 11. "CAB Makes Ruling in Plane Crash" is the *Iowegian* AP headline. The next day a copy arrives by mail to the *Iowegian* office on North Main Street. "Add to the list," says Charlie DePuy, "who think Edward Slattery is quite a man." On the day Slattery, the CAB Public Relations Officer left Centerville, he promised to send a copy of the report. He's kept his word. On August 3, it's published in full on the *Iowegian's* page nine.[284, 285]

The report gives a factual synopsis of the events of the crash and the investigations of the accident team led by George Van Epps. The report's conclusion is short and to the point: "Evaluation of all the evidence leads logically to the conclusion that a dynamite device was placed in the used towel bin of the right rear lavatory with the express intent to destroy the aircraft . . . The Federal Bureau of Investigation . . . immediately initiated a full-scale investigation."[286, 287, 288]

The Nation
Friday, August 3, 1962

Across the country from the *Honolulu Advertiser* to the *Los Angeles Times*, the *Chicago Sunday Tribune* to the *Boston Globe*, headlines and front-page articles are reporting the CAB and the FBI findings.

All report the involvement of dynamite. Some explore "Doty the Deeply Troubled Man." The *Honolulu Advertiser* and the *Waterloo Sunday Courier* report the response of Leo Tanguay the Acting Director of the Civil Aeronautics Board of Safety—a man well-known in Centerville. The FBI Laboratory tests, Tanguay says, reveal more dynamite on the "right aft lavatory electrical junction box cover." It was found in the rear fuselage skin, the interior wall of one lavatory, and the carpet from the aft section of the cabin." The *Kansas City Star's* John Cauley of their Washington Bureau anticipated the findings and his article is copyrighted. At the *Centerville Daily Iowegian* Editor Bob Beck covers the whole story from when Flight 11 is airborne from Chicago to the Shuey Field and after. Charlie DePuy recalls a conversation with the CAB Structural Engineer John Leak. He is still working on the tail section at the Appanoose County fairground building. He tells Charlie the significant place in history of this accident. There have been multiple bombs that have brought down airliners, but every one of them have been in propeller driven aircraft. This one—this Continental Airlines 707-124 Flight 11 is the first JET airliner in the world to be bombed. The words reinforce those of Edward Slattery: "This will go down in aviation history."[289, 290, 291, 292, 293, 294]

September 1962

Sigourney, Iowa
Wednesday, September 12, 1962

Gayno Gilbert Smith is standing before District Court Judge L.R. Carson. His handcuffs have been removed. His shoulders are slightly hunched. He pleads guilty to the murder of five members of the McBeth family, but not in the fatal beating of his stepmother. Sitting with her grandparents is fifteen-year-old Patsy Lou McBeth, the sole survivor of the shootings. She is watching. Smith's attorney, Stephen Gerard, of Sigourney, reads down the list of indictments. On each charge Judge Carson asks Smith how he pleads. "Guilty" Smith repeats five times.[295]

Sigourney, Iowa
Thursday, September 13

Gayno Smith is sentenced to six lifetimes in prison. The sixth is for the death of his stepmother. He stares expressionless when County Attorney Leo Martin asks for the death penalty. Judge Carson, who could have doomed Gayno to death, rules for life in prison and the prisoner "never to be released . . ." not through commutation or parole.[296]

As Gayno leaves the court he speaks to representatives of the press. "I still can't believe what happened."

"I think mainly my whole trouble lies where a person does something before realizing it and before stopping to think . . . If I had stopped and thought about it I wouldn't be in this trouble today."

Gayno is unable to give a reason for his actions. He does give a reason for killing his stepmother. His attorney, Stephen Gerard, said it would not be released.

The weapons Gayno had used in the slaying, the over–under .410 shotgun and .22 caliber rifle, have never been found.

Fort Madison, Iowa
Thursday, September 13

On the same day as his sentence was passed, Gayno Smith enters Fort Madison Penitentiary. He remains there for, as Judge Carson had ordered, the rest of his life. That life ended on May 16, 2005.[297]

Iowa/Missouri Borderland
1962

For all those involved in the crash of Continental Flight 11 there were the expected letters of appreciation from the CAB, the FBI, the FAA, and Continental Airlines. The Director of the FBI, J. Edgar Hoover, wrote to Dr. Judd; so did Missouri's Attorney General, Thomas Eagleton, and Continental's CEO, Robert Six. The FBI leader of the investigation, Mark Felt, wrote to Dr. Judd, "the very efficient and professional manner in which you discharged your duties reflects credit upon you." Felt also wrote to Putnam County Sheriff David Fowler, as did George Van Epps, the head of the CAB Investigation. Van Epps wrote, "During my tours with the Civil Aeronautics Board, I have had the opportunity of meeting with a considerable number of law enforcement officers. Let me say your conduct during the investigation is one of the best I've ever been connected with. Your service went far beyond the call of duty." Continental Airlines CEO Six sent letters of gratitude to the mayor of Unionville, Missouri, Aeron Stuckey, to the people of the town, and to the Unionville Lions Club. He wrote similarly to Mayor Harry Dukes of Centerville, to Father Anthamatten, and to the people of Centerville via Bob Beck at the *Centerville Daily Iowegian.*[298, 299, 300, 301]

But it was the gratitude of the families of the victims that was and remains the most valued, the most treasured. They made contact from across the country, from across the world. Dr. Anthony Owca, at his office in Centerville's St. Joseph's Mercy Hospital, received a telephone call from Tokyo, Japan. It came with expressions of deep gratitude—and a question. Did Takehiko Nakano speak before he died? "Yes" answered Dr. Owca. "He said some words but it was in Japanese and there was no interpreter." From Canada, M.A.C. Hamilton, the Manager of R.H. Windsor, Canada, Ltd., Ontario, gave thanks from the wife and relatives of Philip Hoare the company's Assistant Chief Engineer born in Wales.[300, 303]

Father Anthamatten had walked the entire field the morning the crash site was discovered. He knelt, anointing remains. He found broken rosaries and wrote to the families of every Catholic victim known to Continental Airlines. And they wrote back. From River Forest, Illinois, Tom and Rose McGrath, the parents of stewardess Mary McGrath, wrote that they were so grateful that their daughter received the last rights. Magda Herman, the widow of Fred Herman wrote, "I'm terribly lonely and unhappy Father. My family lives behind the Iron Curtain in Czechoslovakia. Fred and I were so close and so in love. Though I have two teenagers I am completely lost without him." Rosemary, the wife of Maurice Hamilton, wrote that she had no idea how to continue on in life and raise their five children, the oldest eleven years old, the youngest not quite one.[304, 305]

Many of the families came seeking closure at the Shuey Field. The family of Takehiko Nakano came. From Odessa, Texas, the parents of stewardess Joyce Rush, who'd fallen from the tail section, came. They'd heard she fell in a swamp. Dr. Judd and Cleo Webber took them to the spot where her body was found. They were so pleased she had come to rest on the grassy knoll at Kozad Park.[299]

The parents of Mary McGrath came. They visited the site with Father Anthamatten. The Father was chaplain of St. Joseph's Mercy Hospital and on Sundays he doubled as pastor of a Mission church, St. Williams, in Numa. The McGraths presented the church in Numa, in honor of their daughter, and to aid spiritual recovery, a Pilgrim Virgin Statue.[306, 307, 308]

But Father Anthamatten never recovered from his experience of the crash of Flight 11. He was haunted by the scene for the rest of his life. He suffered depression, panic attacks, and talked about it incessantly. He became delusional, having mystical experiences during Mass, and having frightening visitations and temptations.[310]

There were recognitions. Dr. Judd was the keynote speaker at the National Coroner's Convention in St. Louis, Missouri. Centerville's Dr. Ritter went to Ann Arbor, Michigan, on July 19, 1962. He received the Federal Aviation Administration's Distinguished Service Award for "outstanding service" for his work at the Continental Airline disaster at the Iowa-Missouri border. He was the first civilian to receive the award. It was presented by Dr. James L. Goddard on behalf of FAA head Najeeb Halaby. Speaking in response, Dr. Ritter said how in front of him, always, was his respect and conviction towards the dead. "Never in my experience as a doctor have I ever felt like I needed this fortitude as I did that morning because I was cussed, I was damned, I was reported to the Governor. I competed with sightseers, with television, with radio, and just about everyone else there." Dr. Ritter had also sent a letter to FAA head Halaby listing the "deficiencies at the scene." Halaby responded, "You may be sure that steps will be taken to correct those deficiencies."[299, 312, 313]

In December 1962, the Iowa Associated Press Member, Newspaper Editors, and Radio-Television Newscasters, voted the crash of Continental Airlines Flight 11 Iowa's top story of 1962. Two other stories ran for a close second place. One was the election for Governor of Iowa, Democrat Harold Hughes. The other: Gayno

Smith's killing of six relatives. The story of Gayno's capture in Appanoose and Davis counties also won an award. "Capture Murder Suspect Near Lake. Wolf Hunter Pete Smith Finds Trail" by Bob Norberg, the editor of the *Bloomfield Democrat,* was chosen the best news article in a weekly newspaper by the National Newspaper Association.[314, 315, 316]

Throughout 1962 for the Mahoney family in Unionville, the Johnson family one mile south of the border, and for families across the area, every Sunday there was a treat. It was to watch a popular television program, *Country Style Gospel Time,* on local station KTVO. On it, the Guffey family—from Green City some twenty-and-a-half miles west of Unionville, Missouri—entertained and sang their own songs. One song had special local appeal. It was written by thirty-eight-year-old Tharon Guffey who was distraught on learning of the deaths of forty-five people and then she was inspired to compose it. Her song and other Guffey music was copyrighted in 1962 under the title *Earth to Glory.*[317]

1963 and Forward

The Iowa/Missouri Borderland
Spring 1963

Reminders of that night in May 1962 kept surfacing. Spring plowings of this rural land would produce bits of metal, pieces of blue plastic, a frame from a window. Jim Kauzlarich, walking through timber north of the Exline corner along Highway 5(60), found a gray/green piece of metal, a gold knife, a gold key chain, some keys, and some clothing. The name on the gold knife and key chain was Sidney H. Goldberg, a victim of the crash. Jim made contact with members of the Goldberg family in New York City and the items were returned to them. The piece of metal Jim donated to the Flight 11 display at the Putnam County Historical Museum in Unionville.*311*

Seattle
June 19, 1963

One year after Dr. Judd's speech in St. Louis and Dr. Ritter's Award from the Federal Aviation Administration, there was another award. This was a judgment from America's Newspaper Editors—the National Editorial Association. Out of 2,300 submitted newspaper articles from every state of the Union except Alaska, First Place for the best written news story of 1962 was awarded to Charlie DePuy for his story written the day after Continental Flight 11's crash. "At the time the story was written . . . many details were still sketchy and difficult to obtain in the time available before deadline. The story was well-handled and must have had a solid impact on the community," wrote the editors.[318]

Bob Beck at the *Iowegian* knew the full story. Charlie, he said, "wrote it the day following the airline crash under the most adverse circumstances imaginable. He had been up all night. He had to cover the story on his own since other members of the *Iowegian* staff were out of the city, he was interrupted throughout the day by media from all over the country calling him for information. Yet he turned out a story that was skillfully written, full of clarity, that contained zest and vitality, yet gave clear meaning to the tragic accident."[318]

Charlie received his award at a banquet in the grand ballroom of the Olympic Hotel in Seattle, Washington, at the NEA's National Convention June 19, 1963. When he returned to his room he placed his plaque on one side of the desk. On the other side he found a sheaf of telegrams from the people of Centerville. "They took me completely by surprise . . . The kindness of the people who were happy for you means more than the plaque could ever mean anyway." He continues talking to himself, "You didn't win the plaque after all . . . Gladys [Charlie's wife] backed you . . . so did the sheriff and highway patrolmen . . . a hundred kind people . . . the police . . . the hospital . . . the doctors . . . even competing newsmen . . . Mrs. Carl Jones at the Cincy switchboard . . . it was their story more than it was mine. So take a bow. All I did after all was put the words together and write your story."[319, 320]

New York City
1968

In 1968, Doubleday Publishing House issues *Airport*, the fourth novel by British-Canadian writer Arthur Hailey. It's the story of one eventful night at a fictional Midwestern airport. The climax is when a "mad bomber" sets off a bomb in an aircraft lavatory while the plane, full of passengers, is in flight. The novel does not end in the disaster of Continental Flight 11. But the act of the bomber is based on that of Thomas Gene Doty. Arthur Hailey, his wife writes in her book, *I Married a Best Seller*, was a "newsaholic." He read every newspaper every day. He knew about Continental Flight 11. He is also noted for the painstaking research he did for all his novels. In the case of *Airport,* he used an interview with US Army bomb disposal personnel and learned how to install a bomb into a briefcase.

In 1970, Universal Studios made *Airport* into a movie. There were three sequels: *Airport 1975*, *Airport '77*, and *The Concorde . . . Airport '79.*[321]

Unionville, Missouri
October 2001

For nineteen years, after a distinguished army career, US Major Duane Crawford lived in Putnam County teaching science at Unionville High School. He, his wife Kay, and their family lived on a farm north of Unionville. This was when he first encountered the story of Flight 11 hearing how it had "abruptly thrust our quiet, rural community into the national spotlight." He assembled information. He interviewed local citizens, many whose lives were forever altered by the event. Duane's work, his contribution to the history of this event, is too valuable to be measured. Duane published his work in four detailed cogent articles. They appeared in the *Unionville Republican* newspaper 2001, on August 8, 15, 22, and 29, the last one eleven days before September 11, 2001, and the attacks on the World Trade Center and the Pentagon.[322, 323, 324, 325, 326, 327]

When the news broke that September day that "Flight 11" had crashed into the World Trade Center, a young woman in Woodland Hills, California, shouted, "Oh no!!! That's Dad's flight." The young woman was Kathryn Hamilton. Her father, Maurice Hamilton, thirty-nine years previously, was killed on Continental Flight 11 on the Shuey Field. Kathryn was one of her father's five children—the oldest, then eleven years old, the youngest not quite one, and a mother, Rosemary, wondering how to raise these children bereft of their father. Kathryn was four.

In 2001 the Hamiltons learned of Duane's work. Kathryn phoned him. "I've always wanted to come there for a visit and meet the people," she told Duane, "but I didn't know how. Somehow I need to find closure to my Dad's tragic death. I know so little about what happened."[328, 329]

Kathryn came with most of her family. It was the weekend of October 20. The people of Unionville embraced them. There were breakfasts and dinners, BBQs and conversations. They went to the Shuey Field and met Duane, Lester, and Atholene Cook, Terry Bunnell, Lavan Smith, and Dr. Judd, all explaining in detail what they found that morning on May 23, 1962.[5]

Life had not been easy for the family in 1962 living in Cleveland, Ohio. Rosemary told Duane how "Suddenly, I was a forty-year-old widow with no college education. We had limited finances. We learned to budget, make sacrifices and do without real fast." There was no compensation. Except for a sealed casket and a few words of condolence, Continental Airlines did nothing for the families of the passengers. Lawsuits never entered Rosemary's mind, and she never harbored any bitterness against Continental. "It wasn't Continental's fault. The crash was caused by an evil man."[328]

That same day in Unionville, an idea was born: To create a memorial to the event.

Eight-thousand miles away in New Zealand, Andrew Russell, fifteen-years-old and interested in aviation, read a report on his computer: "Aircraft Accident Investigation Report for Boeing 707-124."[330, 331, 332]

Auckland, New Zealand
November 17, 2008

Some years later in New Zealand, Andrew Russell created an Internet blog: "What happened to Continental Airlines Flight 11?" He was genuinely curious as to what he perceived as a gross historical injustice to American aviation—the nearly forgotten air disaster that was the first ever bombing of a jet airliner.[332]

It was one year later on November 17, 2008, Andrew got his first "hit": "Dear Sir, My name is Duane Crawford." That email was the beginning of a remarkable friendship. It was the beginning of a shared objective, to make a memorial to honor the crew and passengers of Continental Flight 11. And it was much more than that. Duane's work and Andrew's website generated a network of contacts for the families, the descendants of the victims. It became a place of healing where their losses, their pains, could be shared—all told so movingly by Andrew in his book, *The Missouri Crash.*[332, 333]

Unionville, Missouri
Saturday, May 26, 2012

On Saturday, May 26, 2012, a black granite memorial inscribed with the names of the victims was unveiled on the Putnam County courthouse lawn. A dream born eleven years previously on the crash site had come true for retired US Army Major Duane Crawford. There were wreaths and family photographs and red carnations brought by Fredianne Gray, Captain Fred Gray's daughter, to honor her father who always wore one in his buttonhole. There was music, the posting of the colors, and the singing of "America the Beautiful." Relatives of the victims and the children spoke of their memories. Andrew Russell, who made the eight-thousand trip from New Zealand, gave the keynote speech.[334]

"When Captain Gray and his crew and the passengers in their care boarded Flight 11 on what I'm sure must have seemed an ordinary May night," says Andrew, "nobody could have foreseen the terror and catastrophe that was to occur aboard a short time later . . . Unionville never asked for what happened here fifty years ago but rose to the occasion to honour that with this memorial and the efforts put into this anniversary."

Talking about the blog he began in 2007, to find information about a crash "so utterly forgotten," Andrew continues: "I had not even expected a single post or reply . . . when emails and posts on the blog started coming in I was initially stunned. Then in 2008 when Duane Crawford contacted me about the push for a memorial I started to realize I had come across something much more poignant than a mere plane crash. What had been initially an historical inquiry became a close connection with Flight 11 as I continued to hear from countless people connected with the flight in some way: people who had lost someone who was aboard, those who had seen the destruction first hand and those who were here to offer support in the aftermath of May 22nd." Andrew concludes, "I only hope that I have given the families some sort of voice to say that you haven't been forgotten, that people still care, that what happened here will never be forgotten."[332, 333, 335]

And so the story is told.

On May 22, 1962, a bomb exploded in the rear fuselage of Continental Flight 11. It killed all thirty-seven passengers and the crew of eight. There were no survivors. But to this day, the people of Putnam County talk of the dog. One mystery remained: a grey and black, beautiful, friendly, intelligent, eager, disciplined young German Shepherd. A dog found at the scene of the crash. A dog with a cut below his chin. A dog that responded to "stand," "shake hands," "sit," "roll over," "come." A dog that was never claimed. A dog who, in a vicious crack of thunder, jumped through a plate glass window. A dog adopted and loved by eight-year-old Robert Fowler in Unionville, Missouri. A dog Robert named Boeing 707.[336, 337]

Postscript

1. Centerville, Iowa, May 29, 1962 note from CAB Senior Structural Specialist J.S. Leak to the *Iowegian's* Charlie DePuy, "the explosion could have been carried aboard in a shirt pocket or a coat pocket . . ."

2. January 5, 1973: At US Airports, passengers and luggage are screened by Metal Detectors.

3. Note: Dynamite—composed of nitroglycerine—contains no metal.

4. November 19, 2001: The Transportation Security Act (TSA) is signed into law as part of the Aviation and Transportation Security Act. TSA agents screen all passengers, luggage, and cargo.

5. March 2010: The TSA installs advanced technology units at US Airports. These are "full body scanners" designed to detect non-metallic weapons and explosives.

About the Author

Enfys McMurry is a native of Wales and a thirty-five-year citizen of the US. She was educated at the University of London, the University of Arizona, and Truman State University. She's taken courses at Iowa State and the University of Iowa's Writer's Workshop.

For seven years she taught in London, England, but for twenty-three years was an English instructor at Indian Hills Community College, Centerville Campus.

She has had articles published in Wales' *Western Mail*; in the US in *The Des Moines Register, The Christian Science Monitor, The San Francisco Examiner, Architectural Digest,* as well as Centerville's *Iowegian.*

She is the author of *Hearst's Other Castle* and appeared on a BBC Television program on St. Donat's Castle, one of William Randolph Hearst's homes, on the coast of Wales.

Her book, *Centerville: A Mid-American Saga,* was published in 2013. It was ten years of research that culminated in a comprehensive history. "Centerville's history is a microcosm of American history and Enfys has captured it in this magnificent book," per the Appanoose County Historical & Coal Mining Museum website.

Acknowledgments

Susan Bruner, writing an academic paper in 1988, first gave order to the conversations I'd heard when coming to live in this Iowa/ Missouri borderland. Susan spent weeks in the offices of two newspapers: the *Daily Iowegian* in Centerville, Iowa, and the *Times Republican* in Unionville, Missouri. In addition she interviewed Dr. Charles Judd, Lester Cook who was with his son Ronnie who found the wreckage, and Norman Brice, one of the funeral directors. But it was another thirty-three years before I began this account. And in that time, there was another key influence.

Rosalie Mahoney, a GI bride from my native Wales living in Unionville, knowing my love of history, mailed me every article written by Duane Crawford. In 2001 Duane's four articles appeared in the Unionville newspaper. Duane's work, his detailed account of this event, and his interviews with those immediately involved in the crash area is peerless. Only at the death of Duane could my attempt be considered. And then I could expand the whole story. First I acquired the Official Civil Aeronautics Report and acquired 800 (redacted) pages of the official FBI Report, biographies, access to the official Hall Engineering maps, more local and national newspaper articles, and many more interviews. This expanded the geography of the account from the explosion and path of debris across forty miles of Iowa to the Shuey field in Missouri, and it expanded solving what had caused the crash by the reconstruction in Centerville of over 500 pieces of the aircraft's tail section.

How can I begin to thank those who helped?

In Unionville, Missouri:
Rosalie Mahoney and her son Michael; Dr. Judd and his daughter Serece; Judy MacDonald and Gloria DeHaven at the Museum; Sheriff David Fowler's family, wife Hazelee and daughter Francine; the sheriff's brother, Bob Fowler and his family, his son Donnie and Robert with the heart touching story of his dog; the Cook family, Ronnie, Marla, and Marilyn; Ron Kinzler at the *Unionville Republican*; Monica and Christy Allen and the Putnam County Library staff; Dr. Betsy Montgomery; members of the Rotary Club; Murleane O'Brien; and Junior Johnson, his daughters Charla and Claudia, the first people to reach out to me as I began this story.

In Kirksville, Missouri:
Blytha Ellis at the Adair County Museum and Librarian Jami Livingstone who found me key articles from Kirksville newspapers covering this event.

In Kansas City:
Dr. John Horner at the Missouri Valley Room at the Kansas City Public Library who checked 1962 Kansas City Directories so my street locations were historically accurate.

In Corydon/Allerton, Iowa:
Jeannie Jackson and Brenda Devore, of Prairie Trails Museum, and their exploration of Corydon's *Times Republican* newspapers; Dave Mason who put me in touch with Carl McCarthy who was in the Waverly Radar Station when contact with Flight 11 was lost; Malveena (Jellison) Stewart and Brenda Gress, herself a writer.

In Centerville, Iowa:

Everyone at the Museum and the Appanoose Historical Society; Leo Craver who patiently tolerated my five interviews, and extra descriptions of his dad's actions from Leo's son Todd; Russ Davis, himself a pilot, explained aeronautical terms to me; and Bill Buss patiently explained the official Hall Engineering maps, how those maps were created, assembling details from Hall Engineering Field Notebooks. I am grateful to Ken Boyer for explaining the process. For the first sound and the first flash in the sky of the explosion that night the accounts came from Jeanne Harrington, Junior Johnson, Sharon (Pavlik) Smith and Kris Koestner. Describing the desperate forty-mile trail search for the missing aircraft began with Al Clark, then on duty at the Centerville Fire Rescue Station; Gene Horn who found a missing wing, measuring it for me across his living room floor in Moulton; Dean Kanselaar noting the highway in Cincinnati, and Ann Young who interviewed her family to describe the Cessna aircraft flown by Byron Evans looking for the crash. Patty Timmens introduced me to Gabe Raskie who found Doty's briefcase and with the Raskie family she drove us, pointing across the beautiful wooded land where Gabe found it. I deeply appreciate the sensitive interview done by Diane Senior, and Sharon (Ervin) Brice, giving me her mother's description of the scene in Cincinnati the morning after the crash. Paul Heffron gave me advice for family photographs and information about Dr. Pat Gleason being on the search. Pat's son Dan supplied a pained description of the crash site. Those descriptions were extended by two members of the Centerville's National Guard: Jerry Kauzlarich, observing the FBI at work, and Lieutenant Tom Thomas, working in a group of three, removing the lifeless bodies. Two medical doctors: Joel Baker and Brad McConville gave me interpretations of medical procedures and conditions; Betty Owca gave me an account of her husband tending to Takehiko Nakano, and so did a nurse, Debbie Wardlow, describing the recollections of Dr. Owca. Centerville Lawyer Jim Milani gave the account of aiding two victims, both of the Jewish faith, and moving them to early waiting funeral vehicles. At the recreation of the tail section in Centerville, Gary Barrickman described the process and Nancy (Niday) Roberts the emotional effect on her of seeing the victims' suitcases and lined up shoes. Virginia Padovan reported to me how she, then a teacher in Burlington, read in Burlington newspapers what was happening in Centerville, her hometown.

The Gayno Smith Story:

Gary Cridlebaugh began this story. Extending it with their own personal memories were Susan (Dooley) McDanel, Barbara (Harrington) Lindberg, Jane Sheston, Sam Knowles, Dan Wilson, Sandra Smith, and Richard Gorden with the account of his uncle William's valor in World War 1, from Private Detective Jim McDonald who is an authority on Gayno Smith, and Bob Norberg the Editor of the *Bloomfield Democrat* in 1962 whose article describing Gayno's capture won a national award. For them all is the knowledge that Flight 11's explosion and Gayno Smith's arrest occurred at the same geographical point . . . separated by 39,000 feet.

And there's more:

Three contacts provided insight into those three pilots. In a chance Facebook contact with a friend in England, we learn the Engineer, 2nd Officer Roger Dean Allen, was married to his English bride in an idyllic country church in England's Suffolk County. The two were about to buy a home in California and about to adopt a child. To Roger's widow both opportunities were lost. She remained in the US, was always cheerful, and never remarried. From Andrew Russell's book, *The Missouri Crash,* we learn the 1st Officer, Edward Sullivan, was proud of his Irish heritage, had a marvelous sense of humor, and was father to a son. From his nephew, Craig Gray, Captain Fred Gray was so in love with flying, he infected the family.

He taught his brother Carl to fly and Carl, for thirty-three years was captain for Braniff International. In turn, Craig, Carl's son and Fred's nephew, caught the infection. Craig also became a captain for thirty-two years, twenty-five of those for Northwest Airlines. Everyone loved Captain Fred Gray. He's described as "Continental's favorite pilot," a close friend of the CEO of Continental Airlines, Bob Six. He was always cheerful and at fifty-one, the father of an adopted child, was anticipating in another four months the arrival of his own. His ability as a pilot was unquestioned. At his funeral a speaker said, "If anyone could have flown an aircraft minus a tail section and a wing, it was Freddie Gray".

Finally there are those I consider friends, always ready to help, always ready to shore up my doubts. They are Jeremy McElvain, Roger and Sandy Griffing, Kris Kesterson, Kerry Cathcart, James Kenyon, Gary Craver who deserves the title "Mr. Centerville History," Dean and Linda Kanselaar, Lisa Eddy—my ever patient and tech-savvy typist—and Linda Fain, a neighbor who is also tech-savvy. Lawrence Chapman in California who I've never met but his support, his promotion of me, is a star in my sky, John my son whose love is as endless as his patience, and so too my family and friends who might live on the other side of the Atlantic but their support is unwavering. How can I be so lucky?

Sources

1. Civil Aeronautics Board, *Accident Investigation Report.* Adopted: July 26, 1962, Released: August 1, 1962. Library Archive: Center for Aerospace Safety Education 1/18/02. Pages 1, 2 of 8.

2. Serling, Robert J. *Maverick: The Story of Robert Six and the Continental Airlines*, Doubleday & Company, Inc. Garden City, New York 1974. Page 204.

3. Chas. B. DePuy, 1963. "Night of Terror Told By Newsman," *Centerville Daily Iowegian*, February 28, 1963.

4. Federal Bureau of Investigation Report of Identification of the Victims, 1962. Contained in Charles B. DePuy, "The Untold Story of The Continental Airlines Jet Crash Here," *Centerville Daily Iowegian*, June 22, 1962.

5. Crawford, Duane, "Flight 11 is Missing," *In Their Own Words Vol. 2* Stories originally published in the *Unionville Republican and Putnam County Journal.* Pages 76, 77.

6. Boester, Ralph. Email to Andrew Russell, author of *The Missouri Crash*, ISBN 9781790441792 counted pages 63, 64.

7. Duley, Tim to Andrew Russell, author of *The Missouri Crash*, ISBN 9781790441792 counted pages 53, 54.

8. Bender, Jonathan. "Fifty years ago this week, Continental Flight 11 fell out of the sky over Unionville," *The Pitch*: Kansas City's independent source for news and culture. May 23, 2012.

9. Craver, Leo. Interview by the author. May 12, 2018.

10. City of Centerville Police Department Radio Station KAA947. Log Sheet Na456.

11. Fowler, Hazelee. Interview by the author. January 10, 2020.

12. Crawford, Duane. "Flight 11 is Missing," *In Their Own Words Vol. 2* Stories originally published in the *Unionville Republican and Putnam County Journal.* Pages 78, 79.

13. Fannon, E.W. "Bunnell Farm Center Of Activity In North Missouri." *Centerville Daily Iowegian*. May 24, 1962.

14. Radar Operator. Caption below picture. *Waterloo Daily Courier*, May 19, 1961, page 19.
15. McCarthy, Carl. Interview by the author. May 13, 2022
16. "Think Clear-Air Turbulence Tore Apart Jetliner," *Waterloo Daily Courier*, May 25, 1962, page 2, 3.
17. Johnson: Claude Junior; Charla Johnson Kepner; Claudia Johnson McCarthy. Interview by author, May 24, 2019.
18. C.B. DePuy. "LAST BODY FOUND." *Centerville Daily Iowegian*. May 25, 1962.
19. Pavlik, Sharon Smith, Interview by the author. January 29, 2020.
20. Craver, Gary. Interview by the author. January 21, 2021.
21. Fowler-Harrington, Jeanne. Interview by the author. September 20, 2020.
22. Crawford, Duane. "Peace Before the Storm: Boeing 707 Airplane crash of 1962 in North Putnam Co. Part 1 of IV." *Unionville Republican and Putnam County Journal*. August 8, 2001.
23. Beck, Robert K. "Publisher's Corner." *Centerville Daily Iowegian*. June 1, 1962.
24. Craver, Leo, 2020. Interview by the author. January 10, 2020.
25. Wales, Lynetta Jones. Interview by the author. September 2, 2019.
26. Pavlik, Sharon Smith. Interview by the author. January 29, 2020.
27. Koestner, Kris. Interview by the author. October 22, 2019.
28. Charles B. DePuy. "FBI Holds Parley." *Centerville Daily Iowegian*. May 29, 1962.
29. Crawford, Duane. "Flight 11 goes down: Putnam County goes into action." Part 2 of 4. *Unionville Republican and Putnam County Journal*. August 15, 2001.
30. "Bonnell Farm Site of Stark Tragedy." *Centerville Daily Iowegian*. May 23, 1962.
31. Sangsted, Marla Cook. Interview by the author. October 4, 2019.
32. Carmack, Marilyn Cook. Interview by the author. October 4, 2019.
33. Craver, Leo. Interview by the author. April 29, 2020.
34. Beck, Robert K. "Weekend Special: Publisher's Corner." *Centerville Daily Iowegian*. June 1, 1962.
35. Halaby, Najeeb E. *Cross Winds: An Airman's Memoir*. Doubleday & Company, Inc. Garden City, New York. 1978 page 124.
36. Clark, Al. Interview by the author. January 8, 2020.
37. Clark, Al. Personal journal. Page 50.
38. "Aviation History in Crash." *Centerville Daily Iowegian*. May 31, 1962.
39. Lorenz, Andrea. "Unraveling the crash of Flight 11." *The Kansas City Star*. Sunday, January 8, 2006.
40. "Little Groups Wait and Wait." *Waterloo Daily Courier*, May 23, 1962.

41. Bender, Jonathan. "Fifty years ago this week, Continental Flight 11 fell out of the sky over Unionville." *The Pitch*: Kansas City's independent source for news and culture. May 23, 2012.

42. DePuy, Charles B. "Jetliner Crashes Here, 45 Killed." *Centerville Daily Iowegian*. May 23, 1962.

43. Horn, Gene. Interview by the author. February 28, 2020.

44. Johnson, Hugh I. "We Also Serve... Air Disaster. Finds Prompt and Willing Cooperation." *Mid-Continent Mortician*. July 1962. Page 16.

45. Johnson, L.J. Interview by the author. May 9, 2003.

46. Buss, Bill. Interview by the author. October 10, 2019.

47. Dr. E.F. Ritter. *Medical Newsletter*. Aviation Medical Service. Federal Aviation Agency. Vol. 3 No. 8. Aug 1962.

48. "Justamere Farm Changes Hands And New Medical Partnership Is Formed In City." *Centerville Daily Iowegian*, January 16, 1946.

49. Bogle, Marijo. Interview by the author. April 1, 2020.

50. Stamps, Maurice. Interview by the author. September 20, 2017.

51. Charles B. DePuy, "Jetliner Crashes Here, 45 Killed." *Centerville Daily Iowegian*. May 23, 1962.

52. Dr. E.F. Ritter. *Medical Newsletter*. Aviation Medical Service. Federal Aviation Agency. Vol. 3 No. 7. July 1962.

53. Kanselaar, Dean. Interview by the author. June 2, 2021.

54. "Cincy Mayor Corrects an Oversight in Plane Crash." Letter from Mayor John N. Atkinson. *Centerville Daily Iowegian*. June 11, 1962.

55. Morgan, Kae Rush. Interview by the author. June 4, 2021.

56. Charles B. DePuy. "Story of Jet Plane Crash Here Wins Top National Award." *Centerville Daily Iowegian*. July 22, 1963.

57. "45 Die in Iowa Jetliner Disaster." *Waterloo Daily Courier*, May 23, 1962.

58. Crawford, Duane. Interview by the author. May 22, 2012.

59. Wear, Hazelee Fowler. Interview by the author. January 10, 2020.

60. Horn, Gene. Interview by the author. February 28, 2020.

61. "Kirksville Personnel on Scene." *Kirksville Daily Express*, May 24, 1962.

62. Carmack, Marilyn Cook. Interview by the author. January 26, 2020.

63. "Bonnell Farm Site of Stark Tragedy." *Centerville Daily Iowegian*, May 23, 1962.

64. Cook, Terry. Interview with Diane Senior. Notes provided to the Author. June 1, 2020.

65. "Lone Survivor Dies; Found Inside Plane." *Kirksville Daily Express*. May 25, 1962.

66. Fowler, Robert. Interview by the author. March 5, 2020.

67. Fowler, Robert. Introduction by Duane Crawford. "A German Shepard [sic] named Boeing 707." *Centerville Daily Iowegian*. May 5, 2009.

68. Young, Ann. Interview by the author. May 22, 2020.

69. "Helped Search for the Plane." *Centerville Daily Iowegian*. May 24, 1962.

70. "Many People are in Town." *Centerville Daily Iowegian*. May 25, 1962.

71. Fowler, Donnie. Interview by the author. March 10, 2020.

72. Thomas, Tom. Interview by the author. June 1, 2021.

73. Owca, Betty. Interview by the author. February 23, 2020.

74. Judd, Dr. Charles. Interview by the author. August 29, 2002.

75. Baker, Dr. Joel. Corydon Family Medical Center. Interview by the author. May 28, 2020.

76. Giglio, James N. *Call Me Tom. The Life of Thomas F. Eagleton.* University of Missouri Press, 2011. Page 111/112.

77. Cridlebaugh, Gary. Interview by the author. June 4, 2020.

78. Wehrle, Mark. Interview by the author. June 8, 2020.

79. "Dr. E.F. Ritter of Centerville…" photograph. *Centerville Daily Iowegian*. May 25, 1962.

80. Pauley, Bill. Quoted in Crawford, Duane. "Flight 11 Goes Down: Putnam County Goes Into Action." *Unionville Republican and Putnam County Journal*. August 15, 2001.

81. Anthamatten, Rev. Joseph. C.P.P.S. as told to Bernadette Demechko. "Devotion Through Tragedy." *The Apostle: A Publication of The Mariannhill Fathers*. February, 1963. Vol. 41. No 2.

82. Charles B. DePuy, "The Untold Story of The Continental Airlines Jet Crash Here," *Centerville Daily Iowegian*, June 22, 1962.

83. "It All Started With the Fine Work Done By The Centerville Fire Department." *Centerville Daily Iowegian*. July 25, 1962.

84. "Man Made Explosion Believed Responsible For Airplane Tragedy 6 Miles Northwest of Unionville." *Unionville Republican and Putnam County Journal*. Vol. 6, No. 45. May 30, 1962.

85. Weather – Temperatures – Rain – Forecasts. *Centerville Daily Iowegian*. May 23, 1962.

86. Gleason, Dan and Wales, Ron. "Two CHS Students Report Jet Plane Tragedy Here." *Centerville Daily Iowegian*. May 24, 1962.

87. "Jet Crashes Near Centerville Believe 45 Dead." *The Times Republican*, Corydon, Iowa. May 24, 1962.

88. Stewart, Melvena Jellison. Interview by the author. April 10, 2021.

89. Gleason, Dan. "Writing about Continental crash of 1962." Email to the Appanoose County Historical Society. May 21, 2019.

90. Beck, Robert K. "Weekend Special Publisher's Corner." *Centerville Daily Iowegian*. May 25, 1962.

91. "Last Victim Found; Clues Still Sought." *Kirksville Daily Express*. May 25, 1962.

92. "Crash Places Load On Toll Operators." *Kirksville Daily Express*. May 24, 1962.

93. "Last Body is Found." *Centerville Daily Iowegian*. May 25, 1962.

94. Wardlow, Debbie. APRN Nurse Practitioner. Interview by the author. July 2, 2020.

95. Milani, Jim. Interview by the author. October 10, 2019.

96. Anthamatten, Rev. Joseph. C.P.P.S. as told to Bernadette Demechko. "Devotion Through Tragedy." *The Apostle: A Publication of The Mariannhill Fathers*. February, 1963. Vol. 41. No 2.

97. Young, Ann and Den Hartog, Mary Jo. *One Solid Comfort* (The Story of St. Joseph's Mercy Hospital). Town Crier LTD Pella publisher. Page 83.

98. Walker, Teddy. Appanoose County Recorder. Takehiko Nakano Death Certificate. August 20, 2020.

99. McConville, Dr. Brad. Interview by the author. August 29, 2020.

100. Charles B. DePuy, "Around the Town." *Centerville Daily Iowegian*. May 25, 1962.

101. Ervin, Joan. "Cincinnati Airliner Crash." *Cincinnati Memories 1875-1976*. Self-published by the Cincinnati Labor Day Committee. Printed by Sutherland. Pages 56-58.

102. Brice, Sharon Ervin. Interview by the author. August 20, 2020.

103. "Centerville Is News Capitol of the World." *Centerville Daily Iowegian*. May 27, 1962.

104. Beck, Robert K. "Weekend Special Publisher's Corner." *Centerville Daily Iowegian*. May 25, 1962.

105. "Paul Beer Tells of Plane Crash Incident." *Centerville Daily Iowegian*. June 1, 1962.

106. Lamantia, Paul. Quoted in "Copy of the Detroit News." *Centerville Daily Iowegian*. June 1, 1962.

107. Felt, Mark and O'Connor, John. *Mark Felt - The Man Who Brought Down The White House*. Public Affairs – Hachette Book Group. New York. 2006 Page 56.

108. Kauzlarich, Jerry. Interview by the author. September 20, 2006.

109. Rev. William G. Hubmann, C.P.P.S. Missionaries of the Precious Blood. Liberty, Missouri. Email to Zaputil, Mary Sue. November 25, 2019 at 8:02 AM.

110. "Cincy Mayor Corrects An Oversight in Plane Crash" *Centerville Daily Iowegian*. June 11, 1962.

111. "Pile of Portions of a Wrecked Continental Airplane." Caption to photograph on page 5. *Centerville Daily Iowegian*. May 25, 1962.

112. McCarthy, Claudia. Interview by the author. October 7, 2020.

113. Raskie, Gabriel "Gabe". Interview by the author. October 25, 2020.

114. Judd, Charles L. D.O., *Reminiscences of a COUNTRY DOCTOR*. No ISBN. July 1990.

115. Baker, Serece (Judd). House Calls: *The Life and Times of Dr. Charles Judd.* Author House. ISBN 978-4389-5745-6.
116. Baker, Serece. Interview by the author. September 23, 2020.
117. "G.R. Coffey, Assistant Director…" caption to photograph. *Centerville Daily Iowegian.* May 25, 1962.
118. Knowles, Sam. Interview by the author. October 15, 2020.
119. Beck, Robert K. "Centerville Investigation Headquarters" *Centerville Daily Iowegian.* May 25, 1962.
120. Van Epps, George A. and Slattery, Edward J. Jr. NewspaperArchive.com – Gary Craver, researcher.
121. Barrickman, Gary. Interview by the author. December 26, 2019.
122. Carmack, Marilyn Cook. Interview by the author. January 26, 2020.
123. Beck, Robert K. "Centerville Investigation Headquarters" *Centerville Daily Iowegian.* May 25, 1962.
124. Charles B. DePuy. "The Untold Story of The Continental Airlines Jet Crash Here," *Centerville Daily Iowegian,* June 22, 1962.
125. Beck, Robert. Editorial: "We Had Good Help." *Centerville Daily Iowegian.* May 31, 1962.
126. Crawford, Duane. "PC Happenings." February 4, 2004.
127. Fowler, Donnie. Interview by the author. October 4, 2019.
128. Charles B. DePuy. "FBI Holds Parley." *Centerville Daily Iowegian.* May 29, 1962.
129. Crawford, Duane. "Investigation Begins Into Flight 11." *Unionville Republican and Putnam County Journal.* August 22, 1962.
130. "Water Rescue Unit Purchased." *Centerville Daily Iowegian.* July 12, 1961.
131. Craver, Todd. Interview by the author. August 30, 2020.
132. Crawford, Duane. "Investigation Begins into Flight 11 Crash." *Unionville Republican.* Part 3 of 4. August 22, 2001.
133. "Flight Tape Fails To Give Crash Cause." *Kirksville Daily Express.* May 24, 1962.
134. "Think Clear-Air Turbulence Tore Apart Jetliner." *Waterloo Daily Courier.* May 25, 1962.
135. "Lean to Theory of Clear-Air Turbulence As Jet Crash Cause." *Centerville Daily Iowegian.* May 25, 1962.
136. Montgomery, Betsy. Interview by the author. May 27, 2021.
137. "Burns on Bodies Indicate Blast." *The Odessa American.* May 27, 1962.
138. "16-Mile March Begins in Hunt For Stewardess." *Kirksville Daily Express.* May 24, 1962.
139. Sweet, Richard. Email to the author. July 22, 2022
140. Beck, Robert K. Iowegian Exclusive: "Development of Explosion Theory." *Centerville Daily Iowegian.* May 28, 1962.

141. "Air Crash Autopsy Samples To Washington for Analysis." *Centerville Daily Iowegian*. May 25, 1962.

142. DePuy, Charles B. "Crash Probe is On!" *Centerville Daily Iowegian*. May 24, 1962.

143. Milani, Jim. Interview by the author. November 15, 2019.

144. Revers, Molly Milani. Interview by the author. November 10, 2020.

145. Craver, Gary (Researcher). https://files.shsmo.org/manuscripts//kansas-city/K0480.pdf

146. Beck, Robert K. "Unionville, Mo. Extends Helpful, Sympathetic Hand." *Centerville Daily Iowegian*. May 24, 1962.

147. Russell, Andrew. *The Missouri Crash*. ISBN 9781790441792. (Counted page 79).

148. Crawford, Duane. "Community comes together to extend kindness, sympathy and hospitality to family members of plane crash victims." 4 of 4. *Unionville Republican*. August 29, 2001.

149. Beck, Robert K. "Jet Airline Disaster Historic Event." *Centerville Daily Iowegian*. June 15, 1962.

150. "These Are The Missouri Searchers Who Found The Body of The Missing Airline Stewardess." Text under photograph. *Centerville Daily Iowegian*. May 25, 1962.

151. "All Victims of Air Crash Found." *Unionville Republican*. May 30, 1962.

152. "Possibility Stewardess Was Burned." *Centerville Daily Iowegian*. May 28, 1962.

153. Beck, Robert K. "Blast is Confirmed." *Centerville Daily Iowegian*. May 28, 1962.

154. "Robert Buss Doing War Research Work." *Centerville Daily Iowegian*. April 3, 1942.

155. Buss, Bill. Interview by the author. February 17, 2012 and November 2, 2020.

156. Reich, Peter. "Hint Suicide Bomb Cause of Jet Crash." *Chicago American*. May 26, 1962.

157. Beck, Robert K. "Editorial." *Centerville Daily Iowegian*. May 25, 1962.

158. Beck, Robert. "Publisher's Corner." *Centerville Daily Iowegian*. June 8, 1962.

159. "Plane Crash Attracts Press Corps." Caption below photograph. *Centerville Daily Iowegian*. May 24, 1962, page 5.

160. Rush, Martha Joyce. Death Certificate. sos.mo.gov. May 22, 1962.

161. DePuy, C.B. "Unfolding Drama In Probe." *Centerville Daily Iowegian*. May 28, 1962.

162. FBI Report. Page 9.

163. Beck, Robert K. "Jet Airline Disaster Historic Event." *Centerville Daily Iowegian*. June 15, 1962.

164. Weather – Temperatures – Rain – Forecasts. *Centerville Daily Iowegian*. May 25, 1962.
165. Barrickman, Gary. Interview by the author. December 26, 2019.
166. Reynolds, Ruth. "New York Newspaper Article Features Angles of Plane Crash." *Centerville Daily Iowegian*. July 14, 1963. Report from *New York Sunday News*. July 14, 1963.
167. "Sheriff Expresses Thanks To All Emergency Helpers. *Centerville Daily Iowegian*. June 4, 1962.
168. Sangster, Marla Cook. Interview by the author. January 28, 2020.
169. "Friend Goes To Unionville." *Centerville Daily Iowegian*. May 25, 1962.
170. Ratterman, John. "Jet Probe Aim On Blast." *Kansas City Star*. May 26, 1962.
171. Beck, Robert K. "Iowegian Exclusive: Development of Explosion Theory." *Centerville Daily Iowegian*. May 28, 1962.
172. FBI Report. Page 351.
173. FBI Report. Page 356.
174. FBI Report. Page 366-367.
175. FBI Report. Pages 91-97.
176. Borer, Del. "Putting Together a Tragic Puzzle." Photograph and caption. *Des Moines Sunday Register*. May 27, 1962.
177. Lamberto, Nick. "Blast Ripped Jet, Bomb Hinted." *Des Moines Sunday Register*. May 27, 1962.
178. FBI Report. Pages 621-629
179. "Explosion." *Unionville Republican*. May 30, 1962.
180. "Murder –Suicide Plot Hinted in Jet Crash." *The Honolulu Sunday Advertiser*. May 27, 1962.
181. "CAB Blames Explosion in 45 Air Crash Deaths: Bombing Hinted in Jetliner Disaster." *The Los Angeles Times*. May 27, 1962,
182. "Bomb Probe In Crash of Jet Airliner." *Oakland Times*. May 27, 1962.
183. "Bomb Idea Grows In Air Crash Probe." *The Sacramento Bee*. May 27, 1962.
184. "Bomb is Blamed in Jetliner Crash." *The Miami Herald*. May 27, 1962.
185. "Bomb On Jetliner See Crash Cause." *The Boston Globe*. May 27, 1962.
186. "Explosion Inside Plane Caused Crash In which 45 Perished, C.A.B. says… Probability of Man-Made Blast." *The St. Louis Post-Dispatch*." May 27, 1962.
187. "Blast Ripped Jet, Bomb Hinted." *The Sunday Des Moines Register*. May 27, 1962.
188. "Hint Suicide Bomb Cause of Jet Crash." *Chicago American*. May 27, 1962.
189. FBI Report. Pages 634, 635, 636

190. DePuy, Charles B. "Local Investigation of Plane Crash Closes Today." *Centerville Daily Iowegian*. May 31, 1962.
191. "Civil Aeronautics Board and Team Completes Investigation Here." *The Odessa American*. May 28, 1962.
192. "Funeral Scheduled Here For Hostess." *The Odessa American*. May 27, 1962.
193. FBI Report. Pages 644 and 646.
194. Iowegian Staff Writer and Associated Press: "Search for Killer in Appanoose Area." *Centerville Daily Iowegian*. May 28, 1962.
195. Cincotta, Patsy. "Sheston Notices Many Changes Since He Wore a Badge." *The Daily Iowegian*. February 27, 2004.
196. Sheston, Jane. Interview by the author. October 25, 2019.
197. FBI Report. Pages 98, 101-122.
198. Niday (Roberts), Nancy. Interview by the author. March 18, 2021.
199. DePuy, Charles B. "Explosion Ripped Tail." *Centerville Daily Iowegian*. May 28, 1962.
200. "Blast Is Confirmed." Photograph: "W. Peterson, of Civil Aeronautics Board (left) and D.C. Valle, also of CAB, examine hole…" *Centerville Daily Iowegian*. May 28, 1962.
201. McDanel, Susan (Dooley). Interview by the author. March 24, 2021.
202. Jim McDonald. Private Investigator. Interview by the author. March 30, 2021.
203. "Gayno Smith In Oral Confession of Murder." *Centerville Daily Iowegian*. June 6, 1962.
204. Gorden, Richard John. Interview by the author and email. January 18, 2021.
205. Gorden, Willie. World War I Contribution at Neuse Argonne. Email to Author. January 18, 2021.
206. "Local Lawmen Hunt Murderer Near Unionville." *Bloomfield Democrat*. May 29, 1962.
207. "Check Possibility of Smith." *Centerville Daily Iowegian*. May 29, 1962.
208. City of Centerville Police Department, Radio Station KAA 947. Log Sheet 480. May 27, 1962.
209. Wilson, Dan. Interview by the author. March 20, 2021.
210. "Iowegian Camera Views Major Weekend New Events." Photograph: J.S. Leak, Senior Structural Specialist for CAB… and George Van Epps, Chief of the Bureau of Safety of Civil Aeronautics… *Centerville Daily Iowegian*. May 28, 1962.
211. "New Crash Evidence Investigated." *Kirksville Daily Express*. May 28, 1962.
212. Beck, Robert. " Publisher's Corner – Weekend Edition." *Centerville Daily Iowegian*. June 15, 1962.

213. "Possible Point of Air Blast." Photograph. *Centerville Daily Iowegian.* May 29, 1962.
214. "Group Hunting Smith Nailed Him In House." *Centerville Daily Iowegian.* June 4, 1962.
215. "Local Lawmen Hunt Murderer Near Unionville." *Bloomfield Democrat.* May 29, 1962.
216. FBI Report. Pages 356-365.
217. Hall Engineering Company, Consulting Engineers, Centerville, Iowa Drawing Number 475. C.A.B. Plat. Sheet Number 1: *Wreckage Location*; Sheet Number 2: *Topography of Site of Wreck*; Sheet Number 3: *Profiles of Site*. Copies of originals at Appanoose County Historical and Coal Mining Museum.
218. Buss, Bill. Interview by the author. October 20, 2019.
219. Buss, Bill. Email February 15, (3:24 PM) 2021.
220. Buss, Bill. Email with photographs. Feb 10 (11:12 AM), 2021.
221. Buss, Bill. Email Feb 11 (2:31 PM), 2021.
222. Boyer, Ken. Civil Engineer. Interview by the author. March 23, 2021.
223. FBI Report. Pages 314 – 324.
224. Iowegian Staff Writer and Associated Press: "Search for Killer in Appanoose Area." *Centerville Daily Iowegian.* May 28, 1962.
225. City of Centerville Police Department, Radio Station KAA 947. Log Sheets 485, 486, 487 488. May 27, 1962.
226. Bulletin – "Sheriff Paul Thomas reporting…" (Front Page) *Centerville Daily Iowegian.* May 29, 1962.
227. "Papers Team On Pictures." *Centerville Daily Iowegian.* May 28, 1962.
228. "The Andy McBeth Family…" Photograph & Text. "House Where Gayno Smith…" Photograph & Text. "Possemen Take a Breather…" Photograph & Text. Centerville Daily Iowegian. May 28, 1962.
229. "Centerville Is News Capital of World Since Plane Crash." *Centerville Daily Iowegian.* May 31, 1962.
230. FBI Report. Page 10.
231. FBI Report. Pages 12-58.
232. FBI Report. Pages 441 – 446.
233. FBI Report. Pages 59 – 88.
234. FBI Report. Pages 313-328.
235. FBI Report. Pages 503-510
236. Staff writers and Associated Press. "Check Possibility of Smith Suicide." *Centerville Daily Iowegian.* May 29, 1962.
237. "Local Lawmen Hunt Murderer Near Unionville." *Bloomfield Democrat.* May 29, 1962.
238. "Senators Told of Metal Particles Found in Body." *Centerville Daily Iowegian.* May 29, 1962.

239. FBI Report Pages 560 – 578 – 584.

240. FBI Report Pages 631 – 633.

241. Harrington, Jeanne. Interview by the author. August 15, 2014.

242. Beck, Robert K. "Local Ingenuity Aids Smith Capture." *Centerville Daily Iowegian*. May 31, 1962.

243. Lindberg, Barbara (Harrington). Interview by the author. March 2, 2021.

244. Snow, Sandy (Smith). Interview by the author. March 8, 2021.

245. Capaldo, Chuck. "Farmer in Big Part in Capture." *Centerville Daily Iowegian*. May 31, 1962.

246. FBI Report. Pages 590 – 609.

247. Norberg, Bob. "Capture Murder Suspect Near Lake." *The Bloomfield Democrat*. May 31, 1962.

248. "Captured in Barn Near Drakesville." *Centerville Daily Iowegian*. May 31, 1962.

249. AP: "Aviation History In Crash." *Centerville Daily Iowegian*. May 31, 1962.

250. AP: "Jetliner Blast Was a "First." *Waterloo Daily Courier*. May 31, 1962.

251. DePuy, Charles. "Around the Town." *Centerville Daily Iowegian*. August 3, 1962.

252. FBI Report. Page 642.

253. Beck, Robert K. Editorial. "Make Complete Investigation." *Centerville Daily Iowegian*. May 28, 1962.

254. FBI Report. Pages 285-303.

255. FBI Report. Pages 637-640.

256. DePuy, Charles. "Around the Town." *Centerville Daily Iowegian*. June 1, 1962.

257. "Army Guards Leave Scene of Jet Crash." *Centerville Daily Iowegian*. June 1, 1962.

258. DePuy, Charles. "Empty Seats on a Farm Hillside." Photograph and caption. *Centerville Daily Iowegian*. June 1, 1962.

259. "Probe Still Goes On." *Centerville Daily Iowegian*. June 4, 1962.

260. "Doty Angle Grows In Jetliner Crash." *Centerville Daily Iowegian*. June 18, 1962.

261. FBI Report. Pages 65-69.

262. FBI Report. Pages 371 – 372.

263. FBI Report. Pages 404.

264. FBI Report. Page 382.

265. FBI Report. Page 509.

266. FBI Report. Page 333.

267. FBI Report. Page 517.

268. "Gayno Smith In Oral Confession of Murder." *Centerville Daily Iowegian*. June 6, 1962.

269. "Where is Gayno Smith's Stepmother?" "Mrs. Smith has disappeared." *Centerville Daily Iowegian*. June 7, 1962.

270. "More Horror Added To Killer's Story." *Centerville Daily Iowegian*. June 11, 1962.

271. "Macabre Addition To Five Keokuk County Killings." *Centerville Daily Iowegian*. June 13, 1962.

272. "Find More Clues In Death of Mrs. Smith." *Centerville Daily Iowegian*. June 14, 1962.

273. "Says Gayno Doesn't Remember Killings." *Centerville Daily Iowegian*. June 15, 1962.

274. *Unionville Republican* Newspaper Vol. 96 #48 Wednesday, June 20, 1962.

275. Beck, Robert K. "Weekend Special: Publisher's Corner." *Centerville Daily Iowegian*. June 22, 1962.

276. Russell, Andrew. *The Missouri Crash*. ISBN: 978-1790441792. Counted page 79.

277. FBI Report. Cover Sheet.

278. FBI Report. Bureau File # 149-2144. Title: "Unknown Subject; Crash of Continental Airlines Boeing 707, Flight 11, near Unionville, Missouri, May 22, 1962." Synopsis p1 and p2.

279. FBI Report. Page 644.

280. FBI Report. Pages 599-600.

281. FBI Report. Page 646.

282. "Say Accused Man Bought Dynamite, Insurance; Then Boarded Ill-Fated Jetliner." *Waterloo Sunday Courier*. June 17, 1962.

283. "FBI Probe Reveals Doty Deeply Troubled Man." *Centerville Daily Iowegian*. June 21, 1962.

284. DePuy, C.B. "Around the Town." *Centerville Daily Iowegian*. August 3, 1962.

285. "CAB Makes Ruling In Plane Crash." Dynamite Plot Cause of Crash. *Centerville Daily Iowegian*. August 1, 1962.

286. "Full CAB Report is Published." *Centerville Daily Iowegian*. August 3, 1962.

287. Cormier, Frank. "Study Confirms Dynamite Theory in Iowa Jet Crash." *Waterloo Daily Courier*. June 22, 1962.

288. Beck, Robert K. Editorial. *Centerville Daily Iowegian*. August 3, 1962.

289. *Honolulu Advertiser*. August 1, 1962.

290. *Los Angeles Times*. August 1, 1962.

291. *Chicago Sunday Tribune*. August 1, 1962.

292. *Boston Globe*. August 1, 1962.

293. *Waterloo Daily Courier*. August 1, 1962.

294. *Kansas City Star*. August 1, 1962.

295. Speer, Ron. "Surprise Guilty Plea By Gayno Smith." *Centerville Daily Iowegian*. September 12, 1962.

296. Speer, Ron. "Admits Killing Stepmother. Life Sentence For Smith." *Centerville Daily Iowegian*. September 13, 1962.

297. "Gayno Goes to Prison Friday." *Centerville Daily Iowegian*. September 14, 1962.

298. Judd, Charles L. D.O. *Reminiscences of a Country Doctor*. July 1990, page 40.

299. Crawford, Duane. *In Their Own Words, Citizens of Putnam County*. Volume 2, Publisher: *Unionville Republican* newspaper. Page 92.

300. Crawford, Duane. *In Their Own Words, Citizens of Putnam County*. *Volume 2*, Publisher: *Unionville Republican* newspaper. Page 90.

301. Six, Robert F. "Continental Thanks People of This Area." *Centerville Daily Iowegian*. June 8, 1962.

302. DePuy, C. "Around the Town." *Centerville Daily Iowegian*. June 29, 1962.

303. Owca, Betty. Interview by the author. February 23, 2020.

304. "Jetliner Crashes Here, 45 Are Killed." *The Apostle*, A Publication of the Mariannhill Fathers. Vol. 41, No. 2. February , 1963.

305. Crawford, Duane. "Hamilton family visits crash site after 9/11." *Daily Iowegian*. May 14, 2005.

306. "Aftermath of a Tragedy." *Novena Notes*. Catholic Publishing Corp. May 17, 1963.

307. McGrath: Tom and Rose. Letter to Friends of St. Williams Church. October 7, 1962.

308. McGrath, Rose. Letter to Father Joseph Anthamattan. June 25, 1962.

309. "Out of Tragedy A Service of Beauty at St. Williams Church." *Centerville Daily Iowegian*. May 10 1963.

310. Zaputil, Mary Sue. Bill Hubmann email forwarded to author. November 25, 2019.

311. DePuy, Charles B. "Revive memories of Plane Crash." *Centerville Daily Iowegian*. November 8, 1962.

312. "Distinguished Service." Caption below photograph of Dr. E. F. Ritter with Award. *Centerville Daily Iowegian*. July 19, 1962.

313. Aviation Medical Service. FAA Volume 3, No. 8. August 1962.

314. "Jet Crash Here is Top 1962 Iowa Story." Donovan, Jack. "Gayno Smith Capture Ranks In Third Place." *Centerville Daily Iowegian*. December 20, 1962.

315. "Mysterious Jetliner Crash Rated Top '62 Iowa Story." Donovan, Jack. "Hughes and Gayno Also Rate High." *Waterloo Daily Courier*. December 20, 1962.

316. "*Bloomfield Democrat* wins Award." July 1963.

317. O'Brien, Murline and Guffey, Larry. Interviews by the author. June 12, 2021 and emails April 14, 2021, April 15, 2021, April 19, 2021, May 3, 2021.

318. "DePuy Wins Top National News Award." *Centerville Daily Iowegian.* July 19, 1963.

319. "Chas B. DePuy, Managing Editor of the Centerville Iowegian as he received the First Place Newswriting Award." photograph (by James C. DePuy) and caption. *Centerville Daily Iowegian.* July 25, 1963.

320. DePuy, Chas. B. "Writes from Seattle – Reaction to News Award." *Centerville Daily Iowegian.* July 22, 1962.

321. Hailey, Sheila. *I Married A Best Seller.* Doubleday & Company, Inc. Garden City, New York. 1978. Pages 157, 206, 207.

322. Crawford, Duane. "About the Author." *In Their Own Words, Citizens of Putnam County.* Volume 2, Publisher: *Unionville Republican* newspaper. Page 111.

323. Obituary: Duane Crawford. *Centerville Daily Iowegian.* January 19, 2017.

324. Crawford, Duane. "Peace Before the Storm: Boeing 707 Airplane Crash of 1962 in North Putnam Co." Part 1 of IV. *Unionville Republican.* August 8, 2001.

325. Crawford, Duane. "Flight 11 goes down: Putnam County goes into action." Part II of IV. *Unionville Republican.* August 15, 2001.

326. Crawford, Duane. "Investigation begins into Flight 11 Crash." Part III of IV. *Unionville Republican.* May 22, 2001

327. Crawford, Duane. "Community comes together to extend kindness, sympathy and hospitality to family members of plane crash victims." Part IV of IV. *Unionville Republican.* August 29, 2001.

328. Crawford, Duane. "Life After Dad – the Hamilton Family Story." The *Unionville Republican.* December 5, 2001.

329. Crawford, Duane. "Thank you… Putnam County." The *Unionville Republican.* October 31, 2001

330. Crawford, Duane. "Efforts underway to establish memorial for airplane crash of 1962." The *Unionville Republican.* December 12, 2001.

331. Crawford, Duane. "Hamilton family visits crash site after 9/11." *Centerville Daily Iowegian.* May 14, 2005.

332. Russell, Andrew. *The Missouri Crash: The Bombing of a Continental Airlines 707.* ISBN: 9781790441792.

333. Crawford, Duane. "Flight 11 Crash… A Renewed Interest" *Unionville Republican*, March 4, 2009.

334. Crawford, Duane. "Internet Blogger To Be Keynote Speaker at Flight 11 Memorial Service" *Unionville Republican*, May 2, 2012.

335. Zagier, Alan Scher. "Missouri town recalls 1962 plane crash." *Kansas City Star.* Sunday, June 24, 2012.

336. Crawford, Duane. "Flight 11 Remembrance Service… Recount Developments." The *Unionville Republican*. April 23, 2012.

337. Crawford, Duane. Introduction. Fowler, Robert. "A German Shepard [sic] named Boeing 707." *Centerville Daily Iowegian*. May 5, 2009.

338. Fowler, Robert. Interview by the author. October 20, 2020.

339. "Bulletin – AP Sigourney." *Centerville Daily Iowegian*. June 1, 1962.

340. FBI Report. Pages 133-136.

341. Beck, Robert K. "Publisher's Corner". *Centerville Daily Iowegian*. June 1, 1962.

342. FBI Report. Page 645.

343. FBI Report. Page 645.

344. FBI Report. Page 27 and 28.

345. Padovan, Virginia. Interview by the author. May 20, 2019.

346. Angove, Rodney. Paris(AP). "134 Die In Weekend Plane Crashes… 130 Die In Crash of Boeing 707" *Centerville Daily Iowegian*. June 4, 1962.

347. "Local Disaster In National Report." *Centerville Daily Iowegian*. February 14, 1963.

348. "See No Link to Other Crashes." *Waterloo Daily Courier*. June 4, 1962.

349. "Worst Single Plane Disaster In Aviation History." Photograph and caption. Centerville Daily Iowegian. June 7, 1962.

350. Felt, Mark and O'Connor, John. *A G-Man's Life*. Public Affairs TM, a member of the Perseus Books Group. 2006 page 57.

351. Wilson, Arden. "Backtrack Smith Trail; Seek Gun." *Centerville Daily Iowegian*. June 1, 1962.

Index of Names

Also from Meadowlark Press

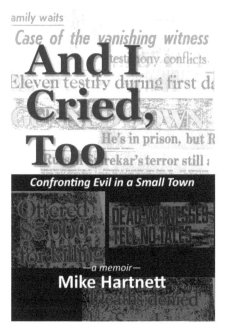

Mike and his wife, Barbara, moved to Lincoln, Illinois, in 1972. The town of 17,000 was charming, friendly, and safe. As employees of Lincoln College, a small, private junior college, they quickly grew to enjoy the subtle pleasures of small-town living. Then the campus was hit with a series of burglaries and a student disappeared. Finally, the murders began. This is Mike Hartnett's personal story, memories that have taken him more than forty years to write. This is not a true crime exposé or a who-dunnit mystery. This is simply a story about one man on the periphery of a series of events that devastate a community for a time. It is a story about the guilt that lingers and the questions that remain.

And I Cried, Too: Confronting Evil is a Small Town, a memoir

by Mike Hartnett

ISBN: 978-1732241084

Available in print, ebook, and audio.

Books are a way to explore, connect, and discover. Reading gives us the gift of living lives and gaining experiences beyond our own. Publishing books is our way of saying—

We love these words,
we want to play a role in preserving them,
and we want to help share them with the world.